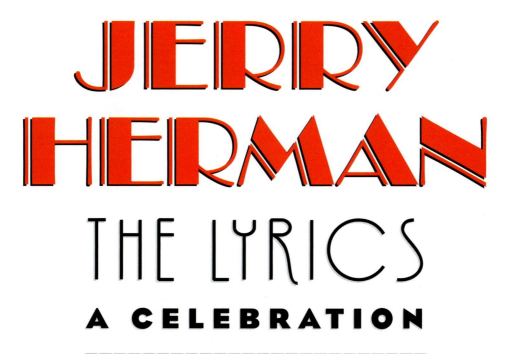

JERRY HERMAN

THE LYRICS

A CELEBRATION

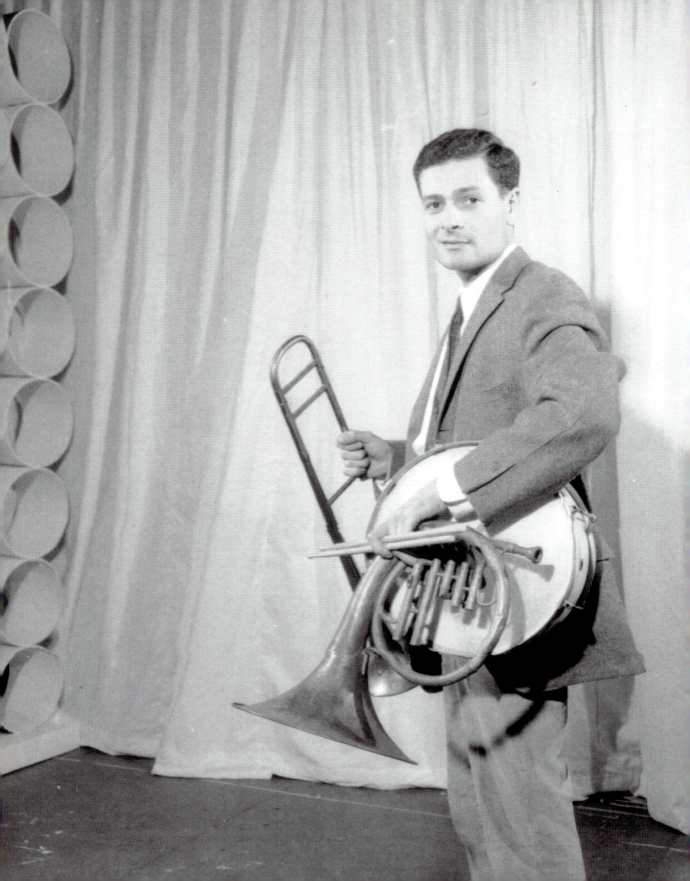

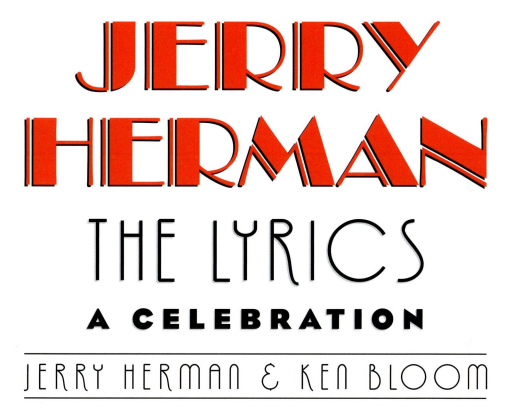

JERRY HERMAN

THE LYRICS

A CELEBRATION

JERRY HERMAN & KEN BLOOM

ROUTLEDGE
NEW YORK AND LONDON

Published in 2003 by
Routledge
29 West 35th Street
New York, NY 10001
www.routledge-ny.com

Published in Great Britain by
Routledge
11 New Fetter Lane
London EC4P 4EE
www.routledge.co.uk

Routledge is an imprint of the Taylor & Francis Group.
Printed in the United States of America on acid-free paper.

10 9 8 7 6 5 4 3 2 1

Library of Congress Cataloging-in-Publication Data

Herman, Jerry, 1933-
Jerry Herman : the lyrics : a celebration / Jerry Herman and Ken Bloom.
                p. cm.
Includes bibliographical references (p.   ) and index.
ISBN 0-415-96768-6 (alk. paper)
1. Herman, Jerry, 1933- 2. Musicals—United States—History and criticism. 3. Popular music—Texts.
I. Bloom, Kenneth. II. Title.

ML410.H5624H46 2003
782.1'4'0268—dc21   2003011580

Book design by Lu Ann Graffeo-Blonkowski/64 Second Design.

Photo research by Frank Vlastnik.

CONTENTS

ANGELA LANSBURY

Some of the greatest moments of my life in the musical theatre were spent on stage at the Winter Garden Theatre singing the brilliant songs of Jerry Herman. Jerry's wonderfully emotional words and music made starring in *Mame* a complete joy.

To have as talented a songwriter as Jerry write a score especially for you is a thrill beyond words. And to have that honor occur on three different occasions is an unbelievable blessing. Having Jerry's friendship is an added bonus.

The lyrics and photos in this book have brought back those heady days on Broadway. I hope that you enjoy reading these lyrics as much as I enjoyed singing them.

And to Jerry: remember, I'll always be your best girl.

Angela

AN APPRECIATION BY

SHELDON HARNICK

▼▼▼▼▼▼▼▼▼▼▼▼▼▼▼▼▼▼▼▼▼▼▼▼▼▼▼▼▼▼▼▼

▲▲▲▲▲▲▲▲▲▲▲▲▲▲▲▲▲▲▲▲▲▲▲▲▲▲▲▲▲▲

Some thirty years ago I interviewed Jerry Herman for a seminar presented by the Dramatists Guild. As I might have anticipated from the quality of his lyrics, Jerry was articulate, candid, clear thinking, positive, and bursting with vitality. Admiring his work as I do, and being a fellow lyricist, I was curious about his approach to lyric writing. Perhaps the most revealing statement he made was in response to my question, "Have you ever done just songs without a book?" His answer, "I'm turned on by musicalizing characters. If I don't have a character, I don't go to the piano." If that was the case, I couldn't help but wonder how he had managed to create his wonderful revue songs (revues being entertainments without narratives and without characters). His explanation, logical and consistent: "With revue material . . . I make up a character. I become the book writer for that day of my life." That the emphasis on character is a hallmark of Jerry's work is amply borne out in this collection of his lyrics. When one thinks of the characters he has written for in shows as different from one another as *Milk and Honey, La Cage Aux Folles, Dear World,* and *Hello, Dolly!,* one has to be impressed and astonished by the breadth of his range. Like a chameleon, his vocabulary changes verbal colors depending on whose voice is singing. To create so varied an assortment of musical voices requires more than verbal dexterity and compositional talent; it requires intelligence, imagination, curiosity, humor, empathy, compassion, the mind of a dramatist, and the ability to express ideas and feelings in both simple and sophisticated language. Jerry has all of these qualities and skills in abundance.

Contrast the graceful and innocent simplicity of "Ribbons Down My Back" with the wry, hard-won philosophy of "A Sensible Woman"; it's hard to believe they're by the same writer. Or take the title song from *Mame* and compare the images that describe the heroine of that show, all redolent of life in the old South, with the depiction of the perky, down-to-earth, Irish Catholic "waitress from Flatbush" in "Look What Happened to Mabel." Each of those four characters is wonderfully alive and wonderfully different. Four vividly drawn human beings with one thing in common: the freshness and individuality of their language. Note the carefully chosen images and phrases (and the equally careful avoidance of anachronisms) are all consistent with the social worlds and the periods in which the characters live and move. Note, too, the sensibility that enables Jerry to create verbal rhythmic patterns that will translate into music as appropriate to its time and place as are the lyrics. (I can't resist adding the title song from *La Cage Aux Folles* to this list of character songs, even though in this case the "character" is the nightclub itself. To read this lyric is to have the club materialize in the mind's eye in full, brilliant detail.)

At the Dramatists Guild seminar someone asked (someone always asks) which came first, the words or the music. Jerry's answer was somewhat surprising: "For me, music and lyrics happen simultaneously . . . For example, I'll get a title idea and musicalize the opening phrase, then skip to the end knowing, for instance, that I am going to end the song 'I Won't Send Roses' with the phrase 'And roses suit you so.' I musicalized that. Then I went back and filled in the middle like an enormous jigsaw puzzle—that's my way. I don't write either first."

The familiarity of Jerry's popular song hits can lead, I believe, to a misleading impression of the qualities that constitute a Jerry Herman song. We tend to equate the name Jerry Herman with the warmth and sweetness of Oscar Hammerstein II, or the clarity and simplicity of Irving Berlin, or the driving show tunes of Vincent Youmans. And, of course, many of his songs do embrace those enviable qualities. But, for me, this collection of his lyrics is a refreshing corrective to that rather narrow view of his work. Browsing through the pages, I found song after song I had forgotten or never knew, lyrics that came as welcome reminders or delightful surprises.

I discovered once again that there are many Jerry Hermans. To name a few, there is the sardonic social commentator ("Just a Little Bit More," "The Spring of Next Year"); the inventive rhymer and master word manipulator ("In the Sack," "Hundreds of Girls"); the sophisticated lyric poet ("Through the Bottom of the Glass," "Garbage"); and the compassionate observer ("Hymn to Hymie," "Mascara"). And as I browsed, I was reminded that each of those Jerry Hermans is a superb, dedicated craftsman.

In the Dramatists Guild seminar, one of the most illuminating responses was Jerry's reply to my question, "Is there an element that draws you to a show, something that you might consistently find in all of your shows?" The answer came out instantly, "Yes, definitely. Positivism. . . . I like shows with 'up' themes and 'up' characters and I will inevitably turn down a show that has a negative hero or heroine." Then he added, "I am interested in positive, uplifting statements that make the audience feel a little better when they leave." There is a risk involved in trying to make such statements. The danger is that what comes out may sound sentimental, naïve, patronizing, or "Pollyanna." Not with Jerry. Instead, he has given us songs that communicate his own passionate belief that life is to be cherished; that, despite everything, life is to be lived courageously and to the fullest. Songs like "I Am What I Am," "It's Today," "Open a New Window," "Before the Parade Passes By," and "The Best of Times" are gifts to be treasured from a generous, unquenchable spirit.

Welcome to the world of an artist whose heart and soul are a veritable cornucopia of song.

Sheldon Harnick
New York, NY, 2003
Sheldon Harnick is the lyricist of Fiddler on the Roof,
She Loves Me, Fiorello!, *and* Tenderloin.

LAWRENCE N. KASHA
presents
JERRY HERMAN'S

PARADE

a musical revue

starring

DODY GOODMAN

with FIA KARIN · CHARLES NELSON REILLY · LESTER JAMES

and RICHARD TONE

Music, Lyrics and Direction by JERRY HERMAN
Choreography and Staging by RICHARD TONE
Costumes by NILO

Production Designed by GARY SMITH

1

OFF-BROADWAY

The off-Broadway scene in the 1950s was a wide-open world of possibilities. Corporations and large producing concerns hadn't discovered off-Broadway yet simply because there wasn't much money to be made in 99-seat theatres. But there was talent itching to show its stuff and a sense of experimentation and freedom in a surprisingly non-elitist community of artists and craftspeople.

Jerry's introduction to off-Broadway came with the opening of *I Feel Wonderful* at the Theatre de Lys in 1954. The show featured a young Phyllis Newman in its cast. It was followed four years later with *Nightcap,* which was produced in the Showplace cabaret. Rita Gardner and Kenneth Nelson of future *Fantasticks* fame were featured along with an unknown Charles Nelson Reilly.

Jerry took the best of *Nightcap* and morphed it into *Parade,* which opened at the Players Theatre in 1960. Charles Nelson Reilly came along, too, and was paired with Dody Goodman. Future lighting designer extraordinaire Jules Fisher, just starting out, lit the sets of Gary Smith; he used carpet tubes painted white as a chief design element (see photos inside). But Jerry knew he was really getting somewhere when Kapp Records recorded an original cast album — and when Jerry was asked, on the basis of his score for *Parade*, to write a musical about Israel. That musical was *Milk and Honey*.

Following *Milk and Honey's* successful opening on Broadway in 1961, Jerry returned to off-Broadway two months later with the book show *Madame Aphrodite*. The show, starring Nancy Andrews, was a quick failure.

Then it was back to Broadway for Jerry and the biggest successes of his career. — K.B.

▲▲▲▲▲▲▲▲▲▲▲▲▲▲▲▲▲▲▲▲▲▲▲▲▲▲▲▲▲▲▲▲▲

Bob Miller and Phyllis Newman in *I Feel Wonderful.* ▶

NIGHTCAP
IN THE SACK

I had a figure problem with the fashions of
    the past
But no more figure problem—now my shape's
    in style at last

In the sack
In the sack
No one knows that I'm poorly designed
I'm a runt in the front
And there's too much behind what's behind
But who knows
And who sees
Underneath my Parisian chemise
Who can tell what I lack
I'm in perfect design
Every fella of mine
Says I'm simply divine
In the sack

I'm a mess
In a dress
With a peek-a-boo split up the side
And I frown on a gown
Where there simply is no place to hide
So blow horns
Wave the flag
I'm the belle of the ball in the bag
I'm the pick of the pack
Since I took up the trend
Every gentleman friend
Says I'm simply the end
(In the sack)

For the new look
I was much too dumpy

I could never get a sheath around myself
For the flat look
I was much too lumpy
But I found myself
When I found myself

In the sack
In the sack
I am burning my old basic black
Each designer I see
From New York to Paree
Wants to throw little me
In the sack

IN THE SACK This is typical of my early revue material that was mainly based on spoofing current trends and the latest headlines. Givenchy had just introduced the world to his sack dress, and so, I ran to my piano. — J.H.

NIGHTCAP
MY TYPE

I am not discouraged 'cause you never
Heard of me
I am not resentful 'cause my name's obscure
Worrying about my lot would be absurd of me
'Cause simple logic makes me absolutely
Sure that

My type is coming back
Fads that have gone their way
Soon find they're on their way back
They've gone through
Plain Janes and helpless mission girls
Oomph, zip, it.
Flappers and Prohibition girls,
Gina, Lena, Donna, Lana
Those who won't and those who wanna
My type is all that's left
Waiting politely can get a girl slightly perplexed
They've gone through you-alls and chic
    chanteuses
Mae Wests and Mother Gooses
My type has gotta be next

Ev'ry little lamb that's lost is being found again
History has proven nothing's obsolete
I can feel the wheel of fortune spinning 'round
    again
Giving me the firm conviction to repeat

My type is next in line
Fads that have fallen are first to be crawlin'
    in line
They've gone through
Wahoo and strut and shuffle girls

Charm, heart, wit
Pure hearted lace and ruffle girls
Girls who please the maharajah, Betty Boop,
    Marlene, Zsa Zsa
My type is all that's left
I'm hanging on to hopes, looks like my
    horoscopes hexed
They've gone through
That Hayworth and Monroe type
What's left but this "miss no type"
The girl's who gotta be
The girl who's gotta be next

THE SHOWPLACE

NIGHTCAP
I WISH I COULD SAY

I wish I could say
Such wonderful words
Instead of my foolish conversation
I wish I could sing
The glorious songs
I sing you in my imagination
I wish I could find a way to free
The dreams I have locked inside of me
But I can only
Hope that your heart
One wonderful day
Will feel the beautiful things
I wish I could say

The beautiful things
I wish I could say

Charles Nelson Reilly in *Parade.* ▶

▼ *(following pages) Parade:* **1** Dody Goodman, Richard Tone,
Fia Karin, and Lester James. **2** Lester James and Fia Karin.
3 Dody Goodman. **4** Lester James. **5** Richard Tone.
6 Richard Tone and Fia Karin. **7** Jerry Herman, Dody Goodman,
Richard Tone, Fia Karin, Charles Nelson Reilly, and Lester James.
8 Dody Goodman.

PARADE
TWO A DAY

It's Nineteen Sixty-one, a time of theatre
    innovation
All commercial gimmicks, all theatrical
    sensation
There's theatre in the park, theatre
    underground
Theatre under sea and theatre in the round
Theatre in a tent, theatre in a pool
Theatre in a horseshoe, theatre on a stool
But all this simply leaves me with a rather
    heavy thud
There's just one kind of theatre for the theatre
    in my blood

For I was born to play the two a day
The hoke, the corn, the empty matinee
And so I know that vaud'villes just asleep
And so I gotta keep on
Dancin' till I rake it up and dig it up and
    wake it up!
I get no thrill from this atomic age
My home is still up on the Palace stage
Where life's a song as long as I can say
I belong to the wonderful world of the
    Two a Day!

I'm only excited and only impressed
By a corny routine in a checkerboard vest
Vaudeville thrills me, how can I ever begin
    to explain
Why a shuffle that's done with a hat and a cane
    really kills me
This current razzmatazz, rock and roll, and jazz
All the noise that people make
How can it possibly compare to the electric in
    the air
When the guy in spats yells "Break … two
    three"

I get no thrill from this atomic age
My home is still up on the Palace stage
Where life's a song as long as I can say
I belong to the wonderful world of the
    Two a Day!

Where I can tell my jokes, sing my song
Show the folks that I belong
To the wonderful world of the Two a Day!

▼ Richard Tone remembers the "Two a Day."

MADAME APHRODITE
THE GIRLS WHO SIT AND WAIT

The girls who sit and wait, and wait and dream
   away the day
Will never know the moment till the moment
   slips away
And then when time has passed them by
They'll look around and wonder why
So, I'll go out and find my love and tell my love
   that he
Was only meant to share his love and spend his
   life with me
And time will never pass me by
For in his arms I'll know that I
Was not too slow
Not too late
"Come follow me" I'll call to all the girls who
   sit and wait

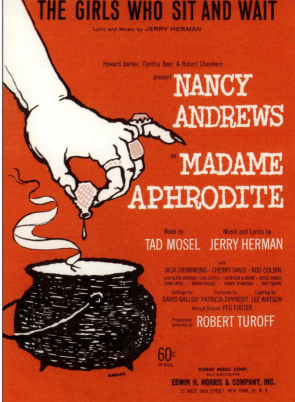

MADAME APHRODITE
THERE COMES A TIME

Sure you're quiet
Sure you're gentle
Sure you're mild
But you look through those bars . . .
And your head goes dizzy
And your pulse goes crazy
And your heart goes wild!

There comes a time
In everyone's life
When something inside you yells "fight"
You live in the dark
You walk in a dream
And suddenly you see the light
And it tells you that
Truth is a fake
And just livin' is breakin' the law
And it says that a pat on the cheek
Can come back as a sock in the jaw!
Life is a trick
And look who'd been fooled
So wake up and kick up a row
For there comes a time
In everyone's life
And the time to haul off
And hit back
Is now!
Right now!

▼ Tad Mosel, Jerry Herman, and Nancy Andrews.

Rod Colbin, Nancy Andrews, and Jack Drummond in *Madame Aphrodite.* ▶

JOLLY THEATRICAL SEASON

Ha ha ha ha
Ho ho ho ho
Bless my soul, good gad
Oh what a jolly theatrical season we've had

Compulsion was such a delight to the viewer
Why two teenage lads stuffed a third down
　　a sewer
And sweet Lynn Fontanne all bedecked and
　　bespangled
Went home for a *Visit* and had Alfred strangled

Suzie Wong's first born is crushed while Susie's
　　selling sin
Oh what a jolly theatrical season it's been

West Side Story has one laugh right after the
　　other
The love of the heroine murders her brother
The brother in order to pay for his folly
Gets shot in the stomach for the grand finale

And *Look Homeward Angel* has a darling
　　deathbed scene
Oh what a jolly theatrical season it's <u>been</u>

I've got to see *Rashomon* so many more times
In every performance Claire Bloom gets raped
　　four times
Quintero's *Our Town* is so joyous and merry
With dead people singing in a cemetery

Ha ha ha ha
Ho ho ho ho
Bless my soul, good gad
Oh what a jolly theatrical season we've had

And dear Arthur Miller still has us in stitches
They're currently burning his *Crucible* witches
The Rope Dancers: how the hilarity lingers
'Cause Art Carney's daughter had eleven fingers

Fredric March got drunk and cursed
While Mrs. March went mad
Oh what a jolly theatrical season we've had

It may not have run long but *Juno*'s great charm
　　was
That Shirley Booth's son had a hook where his
　　arm was
And *Sweet Bird of Youth* is a fun combination
Of dope, hysterectomy, V.D., castration

Ha ha ha ha
Ho ho ho ho
Bless my soul, good gad
Oh what a jolly theatrical season we've had

JOLLY THEATRICAL SEASON There had been a rash of plays filled with depressing themes and ghoulish images on Broadway. So, I wrote a frothy Viennese waltz and sent Charles Nelson Reilly and Dody Goodman on to the stage dressed as elegant first nighters. The hilarity they created is still the high point of my off-Broadway days. — J.H.

Dody Goodman and Charles Nelson Reilly enjoy a "Jolly Theatrical Season." ▶

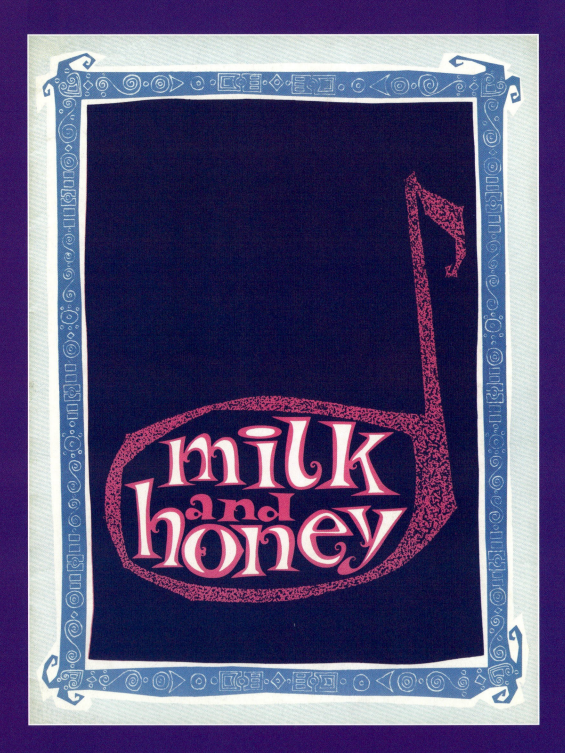

2

MILK AND HONEY

By the late '50s, Jerry Herman had achieved success off-Broadway with three musical revues, *I Feel Wonderful*, *Nightcap*, and *Parade*. Gerald Oestreicher, a real-estate magnate, invited the young songwriter to write the score for *Milk and Honey*. It would be the first Broadway outing for both of them. Playwright Don Appell was also a fan of Jerry's work, and together they conceived the show as a celebration of the then still young state of Israel.

That affirmation of the spirit of Israel was dramatized through its main characters. There is Phil Arkin who has come to Israel to visit his daughter, Barbara, and his Israeli son-in-law, David. He meets an American tourist, Ruth Stein, who is traveling in the company of a group of Jewish widows. The main characters of *Milk and Honey* are Americans who see the new country with the same eyes as the audience.

Robert Weede, star of *The Most Happy Fella*, returned to Broadway as Phil Arkin. Ruth Stein was played by Metropolitan Opera star Mimi Benzell, making her Broadway debut. Also making a Broadway debut, after 50 years in the theatre, was the inimitable Molly Picon, one of the great lights of the Yiddish Theatre. MGM musical singer and dancer Tommy Rall played David, Weede's Israeli son-in-law.

The production opened at Broadway's Martin Beck Theatre on October 10, 1961, to mostly favorable reviews. The mainly Jewish audience took the show to heart and kept it running for 543 performances. The emotional richness of Jerry Herman's first complete musical theatre score was a surprise to his off-Broadway fans. John Chapman of the *Daily News* wrote, "*Milk and Honey* is at its most exciting when Tommy Rall sings a lovely ballad, 'I Will Follow You.' But it was the song 'Shalom' that registered with the public."

Jerry Herman was nominated for a Tony Award for his score. The show was also nominated for four more Tony Awards including Best Musical, Molly Picon as Best Actress in a Musical, Gerald Oestreicher as Best Producer, and Miles White for Best Costumes. The hit RCA original cast recording was nominated for a Grammy Award.

Just as the off-Broadway revue *Parade* opened the door to his success on Broadway with *Milk and Honey,* his first Broadway show led to Jerry Herman's greatest success, *Hello, Dolly!* — K.B.

▲▲▲▲▲▲▲▲▲▲▲▲▲▲▲▲▲▲▲▲▲▲▲▲▲▲▲▲▲▲▲▲▲▲

Robert Weede (milking the goat), Mimi Benzell, and Molly Picon. ▶

SHALOM

Shalom, shalom
You'll find shalom the nicest greeting you
   know
It means "bonjour," "salud," and "skoal"
And twice as much as "hello"
It means a million lovely things
Like peace be yours, welcome home
And even when you say good-bye
You say good-bye with shalom

It's a very useful word
It can get you through the day
All you really need to know
You can hardly go wrong
You're bilingual as long as you say

Shalom, shalom
The nicest greeting I know
Shalom
Means twice as much as hello
It means a million lovely things
Like peace be yours, welcome home
And even when you say good-bye
If your voice has "I don't want to go" in it
Say good-bye with a little "hello" in it
And say good-bye with shalom

It's the most amazing thing
That I think I've ever heard
Wait till Berlitz hears of you
All my foundering's done
I'm a native with one little word

Shalom, shalom
I find shalom the nicest greeting I know
It means "bonjour," "salud," and "skoal"
And twice as much as "hello"
It means a million lovely things
Like peace be yours, welcome home
And even when you say good-bye
If your voice has "I don't want to go" in it
Say good-bye with a little "hello" in it
And say good-bye with shalom

Mimi Benzell, Robert Weede, and Molly Picon. ▶

MILK AND HONEY

This is the land of milk and honey
This is the land of sun and song and
This is a world of good and plenty
Humble and proud and young and strong and
This is the place where the hopes of the
    homeless
And the dreams of the lost combine
This is the land that heaven blessed
And this lovely land is mine

———————————— *sung in counterpoint* ————————————

This is the land of milk and honey
This is the land of sun and song and

This is a world of good and plenty
Humble and proud and young and strong and

This is the place where the hopes of the
    homeless
And the dreams of the lost combine
This is the land that heaven blessed
And this lovely land is mine

What if the earth is dry and barren?
What if the morning sun is mean to us?
For this is the state of mind we live in
We want it green and so it's green to us
For when you have wonderful plans for
    tomorrow
Somehow even today looks fine
So what if it's rock and dust and sand?
This lovely land is mine
This lovely land is mine!

The honey's kind of bitter and the milk's a
    little sour

Did you know the pebble was the state's
    official flower?

What about the tensions, Political dissensions?
And no one ever mentions
That the scenery is barren and torrid and arid
    and horrid
How about the border when the Syrians attack?
How about the Arab with the rifle in your back?
How about the water? What there is of it is
    brine
But this lovely land is mine

▼ *(following pages)* Tommy Rall leads the company in singing "Milk and Honey."

MILK AND HONEY I wanted my flag-waving title song to have a darker side that would give it a ring of truth. I used Adi, a disgruntled Israeli, to contradict all those shiny, positive images. But notice, Adi still ends his tirade with "But this lovely land is mine." — J.H.

THERE'S NO REASON IN THE WORLD

There's no reason in the world
Why you should even look at anyone like me
But I'm so glad you did
So very glad you did
Although I don't know what there was to see

And there's no reason in the world
For you to be here now and watch the days
    go by
But I'm so glad you are
So very glad you are
Although I must admit I don't see why

For there are wiser men and younger men
I wouldn't blame you if you walked away
But I feel wiser now and younger now
And so with all my heart I ask you "stay"

For we have so much more to see
And so much more to say and so much more
    to do
I think you ought to know, if I never let you go
That I'd have ev'ry reason in the world . . .
You!

For there was never time but wasted time
And hardly reason to begin the day
But I look forward now to morning now
And so with all my heart I ask you "stay"

For I feel suddenly alive aware that I've been
    touched
By something warm and new
I think you ought to know, if I never let you go
That I'd have ev'ry reason in the world . . .
You!

▼ Molly Picon, Robert Weede, and Mimi Benzell with the widows.

CHIN UP, LADIES

Missus Segal, Cincinnati
Finds it, oh, such a comfort to believe
Tho' she came here Missus Segal, Cincinnati
She may come home Missus Levy, Tel Aviv
Tel Aviv, Tel Aviv
She may come home Missus Levy, Tel Aviv

Missus Perlman, Jersey City
Has been thinking how lovely it would be
To send home a postal card to Jersey City
And to sign it Missus Cohen, Galilee
Galilee, Galilee
And to sign it Missus Cohen, Galilee

And Missus Kessler found out that Missus
    Strauss
Is wearing old blue garters and a borrowed blouse
And Missus Breslin has been as busy as a bee
Rehearsing an Israeli lyric for "O Promise Me"

Missus Weinstein, Chattanooga
Likes authentic Israeli atmosphere
When the tour is behind her she'd have
    something to remind her
If she carried home a six-foot souvenir

Now Missus Breslin would like a dark roué
And Missus Strauss likes temples that are
    turning gray
And Missus Kessler would like a moustache
    and a cleft
And what would you like, Clara?

I'd like anything that's left!

Chin up, ladies
Look around the horizon
Head high, ladies
Don't give up the ship
Look for the silver lining
You gotta go on with the show
Climb ev'ry mountain
To find your Mister Snow
So always hip hup, ladies
There's a brighter tomorrow
Stiff upper lip up, ladies
Do or die is the plan
Don't ever be discouraged
Don't ever be perplexed
There's always another country
Russia may be next
So keep your chin up, ladies
Somewhere over the rainbow there's a man

With a vevo and a vivo and a vevo vivo vum
With a cheer up an a clear up and a don't be,
won't be glum
With a smile whenever you're able and a laugh
whenever you can
'Cause ladies, somewhere over the rainbow
there's a man

Hup!

Reprise
We only came here to see the Wailing Wall
To watch the Inbal dance, to hear Jehovah's call
And though we came for just a snapshot and a tan
You think we'd start a lawsuit if we came home
    with a man?

Missus Hor'witz from Jerus'lem
And you'll hold out your hand and say "How nice"
Not rememb'ring Missus Hor'witz from
    Jerus'lem
Was the former, God should help me, Missus
    Weiss!

CHIN UP, LADIES This was my first hotel-room song. Molly Picon was such a hit with our audiences that they virtually demanded more of her. The whole sequence was written, choreographed, orchestrated, and put in to the show in 48 hours! — J.H.

THAT WAS YESTERDAY

That plan of mine had the problem of
    tomorrow solved
For I was fine if I didn't have to get involved

But that was yesterday that was yesterday
And it's gone it's over and it's done
For with you my mood strikes an attitude
That's in competition with the sun!

For when my hair was up, my morale was down
I was dull and colorless and gray
But what's past is past, I've come home at last
Where you are tomorrow is, how far tomorrow
    is from
Yesterday

But that was yesterday, only yesterday
And my equilibrium returned
And there's not a chance of a backward glance
Over all the bridges I have burned

For I was someone else in some other time
I was sev'ral million miles away
But I'm back and fine, with your hand in mine
And I'll stay the way I am, how far away I
    am from
Yesterday

Collecting eggs from the chickens even before
    it's light
If I didn't call her for dinner, she'd sit and
    she'd sew all night
She made the gowns for the wedding
Nobody works as hard
It's a good thing nobody asked her or she'd be
    standing guard

But that was yesterday, only yesterday
And I'm in a very diff'rent boat
Working at your side who'd believe that I'd
Ever get so friendly with a goat!

But that was yesterday, only yesterday
But her equilibrium returned
And there's not a chance of a backward glance
Over all the bridges that she's burned

For she was someone else, in some other time
She was several million miles away
But what's past is past, you've come home
    at last
Where you are tomorrow is
How far tomorrow is
From yesterday

Robert Weede and Mimi Benzell. ▶

LET'S NOT WASTE A MOMENT

Let's not waste a moment
Let's not lose a day
There's a short forever
Not too far away
We don't have to hear the clock remind us
That there's more than half of life behind us
When you face a short forever
There's no right or wrong
I can only face forever
If you come along
I can only find my way
If you're there to lead me on
So let's not waste a moment
Oh look, another moment's gone

 Robert Weede.

 Wedding Dance.

LIKE A YOUNG MAN

Like a young man
With a young dream
You will hear me
Laughing at time
I will plow the desert in the morning
With the power of a boy
Guard the border if I have to
In the blaze of the sun, I can handle a gun
    like a toy
I'll make grain grow
Out of nowhere
'Til the gray sand
Turns to gold
Like a young man
Who's young forever
I swear I'll never grow old

I'll build a house in the middle of the desert
I'll give her a young hand to hold
I'll make ev'ry day an exciting new adventure
And I'll never grow old

I'll make grain grow
Out of nowhere
'Til the gray sand
Turns to gold
Like a young man
Who's young forever
I swear I'll never grow old!

Robert Weede feels "Like a Young Man." ▶

I WILL FOLLOW YOU

In my gray flannel suit
In my shiny new car
In my split-level house
With my big black cigar
Can't you picture me?

I will follow you, I will follow you
To what may be a strange and a lone world
For I know I'd be lost in my own world
If you're not part of it too
I will follow you, I am ready to
Go wherever you happen to lead me
Just in case you should happen to need me
All that you'll have to do
Is turn around
For I'll be following you

I am ready to
Go wherever you happen to lead me
Just in case you might happen to need me
All that you have to do
Is turn around
For I'll be following you

▲ Lanna Saunders and Tommy Rall.

HYMN TO HYMIE

Hymie, for seven years I've been good
And you never heard a peep, and you never
    heard a squawk
Hymie, for seven years I've been good
But now I think it's time we had a little talk

How can you expect a woman to exist
When there is just one lonely lamb chop on her
    shopping list
When she's embarrassed by the grocer's
    sympathetic look
As he pastes a single stamp in her green stamp
    book

Oh, how can you expect a woman not to want
To have her dinner at a table in a restaurant
So you'll forgive me if I'm looking for
    somebody who'll
Permanently take me off the counter stool

For when you're two it's fun to see each
    maître d' become your personal attendant
For when they bow and say "a double," you're
    a little like a queen who's holding court
And so I pray next income tax after my name
    there'll be the lovely word "dependent"
So if I want to be dependent—Oh, Hymie be
    a sport!

Because I'm not a spinster
Not a bride
And I haven't got a lover
On the side

I'm not a horse
I'm not a pony
So my problem is acute
For I'm too old for Hialeah and too young to shoot
So Hymie

Ev'ry night I say my pray'rs and close my eyes
And ask when will I buy my toothpaste in the
    fam'ly size
Now you be honest and you tell me how you
    think it sounds
When I weigh in at the laundromat with just
    two pounds

But in my bathroom hear what optimism is
In seven years I never took away the towel
    mark'd "his"
You know I used to think that cooking was a
    world of fun
But tell me, have you ever made a tsimis just
    for one?

For when you're two, to say the least each little
    snack becomes a feast that you can cater
But then you left me, Hymie dear and I've been
    drinking instant coffee ever since
And so I know you'll understand if I should take
    down from the shelf my percolator
If I should use my percolator—Oh, Hymie, be
    a prince!

Because I'm half a fam'ly
Half a team
But still I haven't grown too
Old to dream
I know that once you met him
You'd like this fellow "Sol"
And so I'm asking for the last time
Hymie?
YES?
You're a doll!

HYMN TO HYMIE I was twenty-nine years old and had to think like a senior citizen. A great learning experience. — J.H.

◀ ▼ Molly Picon.

AS SIMPLE AS THAT

If you're here, then I'm here
It's really as simple as that
If it's your home, it's my home
My world is where you are, wherever we
    two are
Don't ask me to leave you
For this is the answer I'll give:
If you're here, then I'm here
I'm with you as long as I live
It's as simple as that
Just as simple as that

Mimi Benzell. ▶

FINALE ACT II

There's a short forever
That begins tonight
And a long tomorrow
Till the time is right

But you'll hear the doorbell ring
And you'll look and there'll I'll be
You see, a short forever with you
Is long enough for me

Shalom, shalom, you'll find shalom
The nicest greeting you know
It means "bonjour," "salud," and "skoal"
And twice as much as "hello"
It means a million lovely things
Like "Peace be yours," "Welcome home"
And even when you say good-bye
If your voice has "I don't want to go" in it
Say "good-bye" with a little "hello" in it…

CURTAIN

▼ Jerry Herman and Don Appell in front of the Martin Beck Theatre.

Molly Picon held aloft in the "Independence Day Hora."

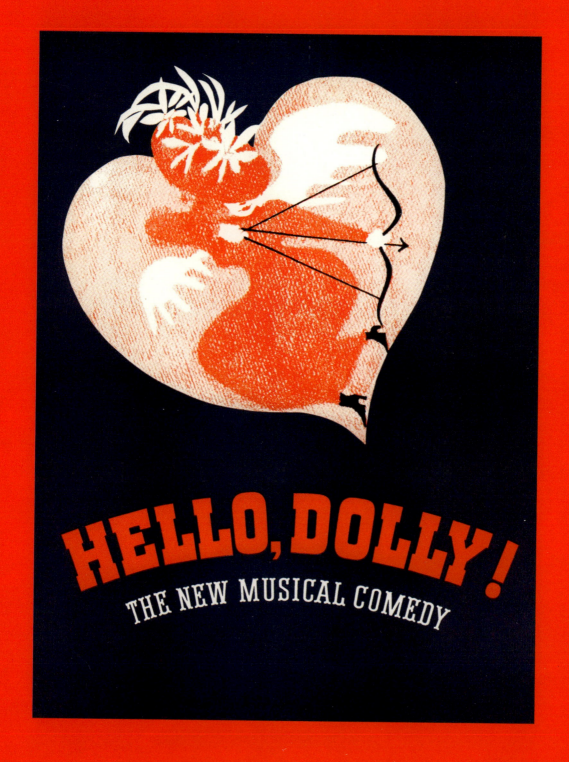

3

HELLO, DOLLY!

Producer David Merrick saw enormous promise in Jerry Herman's score for *Milk and Honey*. The producer was planning a musical version of Thornton Wilder's 1954 play, *The Matchmaker*. That play was a revision of Wilder's 1938 farce, *The Merchant of Yonkers*. The titles alone show the shift in emphasis from the character of Horace Vandergelder to Dolly Gallagher Levi. But Wilder didn't originate the plot. He based his work on two plays: *Einen Jux Will er Sich Machen* by Austrian playwright Johann Nestroy (1842), which was a rewriting of the 1835 English comedy, *A Day Well Spent* by John Oxenford.

While Merrick acknowledged Jerry's talents, he wasn't sure that the young composer could write anything other than the type of music in *Milk and Honey*. So, Jerry took librettist Michael Stewart's script and spent a weekend writing songs on spec. Upon hearing Jerry's songs, Merrick announced that he was hired.

HELLO, DOLLY!

With a libretto by Michael Stewart and direction and choreography entrusted to Gower Champion, Merrick put the new show into production under the title *Dolly: A Damned Exasperating Woman*. Casting for the leading role of Dolly proved to be difficult. Ethel Merman was sought after as the lead and Jerry wrote some songs with her in mind. When she bowed out, so too went the songs written for her. Both Merman and the songs would make a late appearance in the run of *Dolly!*

Immediately thereafter, Carol Channing undertook the part accompanied by David Burns as Vandergelder, Eileen Brennan, Sondra Lee, and *Parade*'s alumnus, Charles Nelson Reilly. Upon its opening on Broadway at the St. James Theatre on January 16, 1964, the show, by now titled *Hello, Dolly!* after its splendid title song, was a smash hit.

Jerry Herman's score, Champion's brilliant staging, Stewart's witty libretto, and Channing's flawless performance all contributed to the 2,844 performance run. Also helping the run was Louis Armstrong's sensational recording of the title song, which he recorded before the show even reached New York. The original cast album sold an astonishing 80,000 copies in its first week on the market. And will anyone of a certain age ever forget the clever use of the title song for Lyndon Johnson's presidential campaign?

Once Channing left the show, producer Merrick engaged a notable list of subsequent Dollys: Ginger Rogers, Martha Raye, Betty Grable, Pearl Bailey, Phyllis Diller, and Ethel Merman (along with the two songs

Carol and I instantly became lifelong friends and her loyalty and devotion to *Hello, Dolly!* will never be equalled. — J.H.

HELLO, DOLLY!

Jerry had written for her). Merrick breathed new life in the show with the casting of Pearl Bailey and Cab Calloway along with an almost all-black cast. It wasn't simply a stunt; the show was remarkably energized by the new production.

Dolly! received the New York Drama Critics Award as well as the Grammy Award for best song of the year (the title song, of course). It won Tony Awards for Best Musical, Jerry Herman, Michael Stewart, Gower Champion (two awards – for choreography and for direction), David Merrick, Carol Channing, set designer Oliver Smith, costume designer Freddy Wittop, and musical director Shepard Coleman. The show's ten wins was a Tony Award record that held until *The Producers* overtook it in 2001.

Subsequent productions throughout the world saw a plenitude of great actresses undertaking the title role. Mary Martin toured Vietnam with the show and opened it at the Drury Lane Theatre in London. French star Annie Cordy made a hit of the show in Paris. And back in the United States, Eve Arden made a notable Dolly, as did Dorothy Lamour, Yvonne DeCarlo, and JoAnne Worley. In 1969, with the show still going strong on Broadway, Barbra Streisand and Walter Matthau headed an elaborate film adaptation of the musical (with Jerry penning a new song especially for Streisand). The film was nominated for seven Academy Awards and won three. — K.B.

▲▲▲▲▲▲▲▲▲▲▲▲▲▲▲▲▲▲▲▲▲▲▲▲▲▲▲▲

◄ Carol Channing sings "So Long Dearie."
This was an early costume for the number but it was cut as Carol didn't have time to change into the dress.

OPENING

Call on Dolly
She's the one the spinsters recommend
Just name the kind of man your sister wants
And she'll snatch him up
Don't forget to bring your maiden aunts
And she'll match 'em up
Call on Dolly
If your eldest daughter needs a friend

▲ Jan LaPrade and Bonnie Mathis horsing around.

I PUT MY HAND IN

I have always been a woman who arranges
    things
For the pleasure and the profit it derives
I have always been a woman who arranges
    things
Like furniture and daffodils and lives!

When a man with a timid tongue meets a girl
    with a diffident air
Why should the tortured creatures beat around
    the bush
When heaven knows Mother Nature always
    needs a little push!
So I put my hand in here, I put my hand in
    there

And a girl over six foot three loves a man who
    comes up to her ear
Surely it's obvious she'll never be seduced
'Til some kind soul condescends to give her
    beau a little boost
So I put my hand in there, I put my hand in
    here

I have always been a woman who arranges
    things
It's my duty to assist the Lord above
I have always been a woman who arranges
    things
Like luncheon parties, poker games, and love

My aplomb at cosmetic art turned a frump to a
    trump lady fair
She had a countenance a little bit like Scrooge
But oh, today you would swear the Lord himself
    applied the rouge!
When I put my hand in here, I put my hand in
    there

And twist a little, stir a little, him a little, her a
    little
Shape a little, mold a little, some poor chap
    gets sold a little
When I use my fist a little, some young bride
    gets kissed a little
Pressure with the thumbs, matrimony comes
When I put my hand in there

For when my little pinky wiggles some young
    maiden gets the giggles
Then I make my knuckles active. "My," he
    says. "She's so attractive"
Then I move my index digit and they both
    begin to fidget
Then I clench my palm. The preacher reads a
    psalm
When I put my hand in there!

I PUT MY HAND IN   The first song I wrote for *Dolly!* I tried to capture her garrulous and nonstop energy by writing long, complicated lyric lines that defined her as a warm-hearted meddler who would just not shut up! — J.H.

▼ Betty Grable sings "I Put My Hand In."

IT TAKES A WOMAN

It takes a woman all powdered and pink
To joyously clean out the drain in the sink
And it takes an angel with long golden lashes
And soft Dresden fingers for dumping the
   ashes

Yes, it takes a woman, a dainty woman
A sweetheart, a mistress, a wife
O yes, it takes a woman, a fragile woman
To bring you the sweet things in life

The frail young maiden who's constantly there
For washing and blueing and shoeing the mare
And it takes a female for setting the table
And weaning the Guernsey and cleaning the
   stable

Yes, it takes a woman, a dainty woman
A sweetheart, a mistress, a wife
O yes, it takes a woman, a fragile woman
To bring you the sweet things in life

And so she'll work until infinity
Three cheers for femininity
Rah! rah! rah! Rah! rah! rah!
F – E – M – I – T – Y

And in the winter she'll shovel the ice
And lovingly set out the traps for the mice
She's a joy and treasure for practically speaking
To whom can you turn when the plumbing is
   leaking?

To that dainty woman, that fragile woman
That sweetheart, that mistress, that wife
O yes, it takes a woman
A husky woman
To bring you the sweet things in life!

▲ Cab Calloway rehearsing "It Takes a Woman."

▲ Charles Nelson Reilly, Carol Channing, Alice Playten, and
Igors Gavon in "Put on Your Sunday Clothes."

PUT ON YOUR SUNDAY CLOTHES

Out there
There's a world outside of Yonkers
'Way out there beyond this hick town, Barnaby
There's a slick town, Barnaby

Out there
Full of shine and full of sparkle
Close your eyes and see it glisten, Barnaby
Listen, Barnaby!

Put on your Sunday clothes, there's lots of
world out there
Get out the brilliantine and dime cigars
We're gonna find adventure in the evening air
Girls in white in a perfumed night, where the
lights are bright as the stars!
Put on your Sunday clothes, we're gonna ride
through town
In one of those new horse-drawn open cars
We'll see the shows at Delmonico's and we'll
close the town in a whirl
And we won't come home until we've kissed
a girl

Put on your Sunday clothes when you feel
down and out
Strut down the street and have your picture
took
Dressed like a dream, your spirits seem to turn
about
That Sunday shine is a certain sign that you
feel as fine as you look!
Beneath your parasol the world is all a smile
That makes you feel brand new down to your
toes
Get out your feathers, your patent leathers, your
beads and buckles and bows
For there's no blue Monday in your Sunday
clothes

Beneath your bowler brim the world's a
simple song
A lovely lilt that makes you tilt your nose
Get out your slickers, your flannel knickers,
your red suspenders, and hose
For there's no blue Monday in your Sunday
clothes

Ermengarde, stop sniveling, don't cry on the
valises!
Ambrose, let me hear that tonic chord
Ahh ahh ahh
Lovely, you're improving. Now, get all eleven
pieces
We're seven minutes late!
All aboard!
All aboard! All aboard! All aboard! All aboard!

Put on your Sunday clothes there's lots of world
out there
Put on your silk cravat and patent shoes
We're gonna find adventure in the evening air
To town we'll trot to a smokey spot where the
girls are hot as a fuse
Put on your silk high hat and at the turned
up cuff
We'll wear a hand made grey suede buttoned
glove
We'll join the Astors at Tony Pastor's, and this
I'm positive of
That we won't come home until we fall in love

PUT ON YOUR SUNDAY CLOTHES
I love the internal rhymes and alliteration, for example, "Get out your feathers, your patent leathers, your beads and buckles and bows." — J.H.

▼ *(following pages)* Jack Crowder, Sherri "Peaches" Brewer, Pearl Bailey, and Roger Lawson in "Put On Your Sunday Clothes."

RIBBONS DOWN MY BACK

I'll be wearing ribbons down my back this summer
Blue and green and streaming in the yellow sky
So if someone special comes my way this summer
He might notice me passing by

And so, I'll try to make it easier to find me
In the stillness of July
Because a breeze might stir a rainbow up
    behind me
That might happen to catch the gentleman's eye

And he might smile and take me by the hand
    this summer
Making me recall how lovely love can be
And so, I will proudly wear ribbons down my back
Shining in my hair, that he might notice me

▲ Carol Channing teaches Charles Nelson Reilly "Dancing."

▲ Emily Yancy with ribbons down her back.

Eileen Brennan. ▶

DANCING

Put your hand on her waist and stand
With her right in your left hand
And, one two three, one two three, one two three
Look, I'm dancing

Take the someone whose arms you're in
Hold on to her tight, and spin
And one two three, one two three, one two three
Look, I'm dancing

Turn around and turn around
Try floating through the air
Can't you be a little more aesthetic?
Don't you think my dancing has a polish and a flair?
The word I think I'd use is athletic!

Well, my heart is about to burst
My head is about to pop
And now that I'm dancing
Who cares if I ever stop

Glide and step and then step and glide
And ev'ryone stand aside

You could learn to polka if you worked a week or so
Or the tango filled with passion seething

I might join the chorus of the Castle Garden show

Whatever you do, for God's sake, keep breathing

For my heart is about to burst
My head is about to pop
And now that I'm dancing who cares if we ever stop!

When there's someone you hardly know
And wish you were closer to
Remember that he can be near to you
While you're dancing

Though you've only just said "hello"
He's suddenly someone who
Can make all your daydreams appear to you
While you're dancing

Make the music weave a spell
Whirl away your worry
Things look almost twice as well
When they're slightly blurry!

As around and around you go
Your spirits will hit the top
And now that we're dancing
Who cares if we ever stop!

Unused Lyric
When the world's in a minor key
And life is a trifle blah
Just find any Alice or Annie
And take her dancing

Don't just sit and say, "C'est la vie"
Say, "Play me that oom-pah-pah"
Get up and get off of your fanny
And take her dancing

Make the music weave a spell
Whirl away your worry
Things look almost twice as well
When they're slightly blurry!

Find a partner and follow me
And sway to your fav'rite song
As long as you're dancing,
The world seems to dance along

BEFORE THE PARADE PASSES BY

Before the parade passes by
I'm gonna get in step
While there's still time left

Before the parade passes by
Before it all moves on
And only I'm left
[Trumpet . . . .]
While I have one
"I'm still in my prime" left . . .

Before the parade passes by
I'm gonna go and taste Saturday's high life
Before the parade passes by
I'm gonna get some life back into my life
I'm ready to move out in front, I've had enough
     of just passing by life
With the rest of them, with the best of them, I
     can hold my head up high!
For I've got a goal again
I've got a drive again
I'm gonna feel my heart coming alive again
Before the parade passes by

Look at that crowd up ahead
Listen and hear that brass harmony growing
Look at that crowd up ahead
Pardon me if my old spirit is showing
All of those lights over there
Seem to be telling me where I'm going
When the whistles blow and the cymbals crash
     and the sparklers light the sky
I'm gonna raise the roof
I'm gonna carry on
Give me an old trombone, give me an old baton
Before the parade passes by!

BEFORE THE PARADE PASSES BY My proudest moment. It was written during a blizzard on a tinny upright in my Detroit hotel room in the middle of the night, under unbelievable pressure from David Merrick. It became the perfect prelude to Dolly's return to the human race, and because it was written specifically for Carol Channing, her comfort level allowed her to belt the song to the last row of the St. James's balcony. — J.H.

▼ Loring Smith and Mary Martin in "Before the Parade Passes By" at London's Drury Lane Theatre.

Pearl Bailey | Ethel Merman
Martha Raye | Eve Arden

Betty Grable | Phyllis Diller
Mary Martin | Dorothy Lamour

HELLO, DOLLY!

Hello, Harry, well, hello, Louis
It's so nice to be back home where I belong
You're lookin' swell, Danny, I can tell, Manny
You're still glowin', you're still crowin', you're
    still goin' strong
I feel the room swayin' for the band's playin'
One of my old fav'rite songs from way back
    when
So, bridge that gap, fellas
Find me an empty lap, fellas
Dolly'll never go away again!

Hello, Dolly, well, hello, Dolly
It's so nice to have you back where you belong
You're lookin' swell, Dolly, we can tell, Dolly
You're still glowin', you're still crowin', you're
    still goin' strong
We feel the room swayin' for the band's playin'
One of your old fav'rite songs from way back
    when
So, here's my hat, fellas
I'm stayin' where I'm at, fellas
Promise you'll never go away again!

I went away from the lights of Fourteenth
    Street
And into my personal haze
But now that I'm back in the lights of
    Fourteenth Street
Tomorrow will be brighter than the good old days

Glad to see you, Hank, let's thank my lucky star
You're looking great, Stanley, lose some weight,
    Stanley?
Dolly's overjoyed and overwhelmed and over par

Golly gee, fellas, find me a vacant knee, fellas
Dolly'll never go away again

Well, well, hello, Dolly, well, hello, Dolly
It's so nice to have you back where you belong
You're lookin' swell, Dolly, we can tell, Dolly
You're still glowin', you're still crowin', you're
    still goin' strong

I hear the ice tinkle, see the lights twinkle
And I still get glances from you handsome men
So, wa, wa, wow, fellas
Look at the old girl now, fellas
Dolly'll never go away again!

HELLO, DOLLY! The song begins, "Hello, Harry" (Harry was my father) "well, hello Louis" (Louis was my uncle, as was Manny). I purposely created homespun phrases like "It's so nice to have you back where you belong" to make the song warm and accessible, because here I was dealing with the very heart of what Thornton Wilder wrote his play about, a woman's return to the human race. When Carol Channing's luminous performance and Gower Champion's brilliantly simple staging were added, audiences all over the world were moved without even knowing why. — J.H.

COME AND BE MY BUTTERFLY

Whenever inspiration fails me
And the city life confuses
I always cure whatever ails me
Just by following the Muses

To a shady glade where the elves abide
Where the water sprites and the nymphs reside

But, oh, the twilight of the evening
Is my fav'rite time of all
That's when the lovely winged creatures
All politely come to call

They call, oh,

Won't you come and be my butterfly
And fly away with me?
On a pink petunia pillow
We will dream away the day
While the naughty pussy willow
And the sly calla lily tickle us silly
If you'd come and be my butterfly
I'd be your honeybee
And we'd flutter thru the pollen
To the song the bluebell sings, ah, ah, ah,
Won't you come and be my butterfly
And merrily try
Ah
Merrily try your wings

▲ David Burns warns the girls, "Watch those feelers, miss" in "Come and Be My Butterfly."

COME AND BE MY BUTTERFLY A pastiche of an 1890s popular song that was used as the entertainment at the Harmonia Gardens. Vandergelder, chasing after his niece, gets caught in a sea of girls in silk butterfly wings. It was replaced by a bland polka contest and I have always missed it. — J.H.

IT ONLY TAKES A MOMENT

It only takes a moment
For your eyes to meet and then
Your heart knows in a moment
You will never be alone again
I held her for an instant
But my arms felt sure and strong
It only takes a moment
To be loved a whole life long

I've heard it said
That love must grow
That to be sure, you must be slow
I saw your smile, and now I know
I'll listen to just my heart
That smile made me trust my heart

For I held her for an instant
But my arms felt sure and strong
It only takes a moment
To be loved a whole life long

And that is all
That love's about
And we'll recall
When time runs out
That it only took a moment
To be loved a whole life long

▼ Carol Channing enjoys a dinner at the Harmonia Gardens.

SO LONG, DEARIE

Good-bye, good-bye, good-bye
Good-bye, good-bye good-bye
Don't try to stop me, Horace, please

Wave your little hand and whisper "So long,
    dearie
You ain't gonna see me anymore"
But when you discover that your life is dreary
Don't you come a-knockin' at my door

For I'll be all dolled up and singin' that song
That says "You dog, I told you so"
So, wave your little hand and whisper "So long,
    dearie"
Dearie should have said "So long" so long ago

Because you treated me so rotten and rough
I've had enough of feelin' low
So, wave your little hand and whisper "So long,
    dearie"
Dearie should have said "So long" so long ago

For I can hear that choo-choo callin' me on
To a fancy new address
Yes, I can hear that choo-choo callin' me on
On board that "Happiness Express"

I'm gonna learn to dance and drink and smoke
    a cigarette
I'm goin' as far away from Yonkers as a girl
    can get

(spoken) And on those cold winter nights, Horace
You can snuggle up to your cash register
It's a little lumpy, but it rings
Don't come a knockin'

I'll be all dolled up and singin' that song
That says "You dog, I told you so"
So, Horace, you will find your life a sad, old
    story
When you see your Dolly shuffle off to glory

Oh, I should have said "So long"
So long ago

◀ A trio of "So Long, Dearie": Betty Grable *(left)*;
Ethel Merman and Pearl Bailey *(following pages)*.

PENNY IN MY POCKET

I studied long division
By the light of kerosene
Economics and the golden rule
Each day I swam the rapids
In a dangerous ravine
Just to get me back and forth to school
And ev'ry afternoon I chopped the wood and
    tilled the soil
And only got a shiny
Copper penny for my toil
But poverty could run no interference
With the Vandergelder perseverance

I put that penny in my pocket
And in a little time
That penny in my pocket
Had turned into a dime
And in a little longer
A quarter jingled out
I put the quarter in the teapot
And waited till the teapot
Had a dollar in the spout!
I put that penny in my mattress
And had some pleasant dreams
Till suddenly my mattress
Was bursting at the seams
And that's how I acquired
The wealth I now possess
But in my pocket is that penny
Yes, that shiny little penny
It's that penny is the secret of my success!

I had a penny in my pocket
And not another sou
And with my only shirttail
I shined a rich man's shoe
He threw me down a nickel
Admiring my skill
I gave my nickel to a blind man
And the blind man left me all his meager
    savings in his will
I bought myself a wagon
And started hauling ice
I cut the ice to ice cubes
And got a higher price
I crushed the cubes to ices
For still a higher fee
A big tycoon said
"Very enterprising in your organizing
Son, you must come work for me!"
En route to work next morning
I helped a lady cross
The lady was—you guessed it—
The mother of the boss
The boss said
"You're promoted
I need you at my side"
And then I met the boss' daughter
And I wed the boss' daughter
And quite suddenly she died
I bought myself an acre
A silo and a steed
All Yonkers started buying
Grain and hay and feed
And now I've half a million
But proudly I confess
That in my pocket is that penny
Yes, that shiny little penny
It's that penny that's the secret of my success!

▲ David Burns as Horace Vandergelder.

PENNY IN MY POCKET Vandergelder's symposium on high finance was turned into a magnificently staged production number by Gower Champion. However, we all agreed that cutting it would make the first act race along and so it was only heard for a few weeks in Detroit. — J.H.

WORLD TAKE ME BACK

I've sliced my slice of life a little thin
Haven't I, Ephraim?
I've been on the outside lookin' in
Haven't I, Ephraim?

The world is full of wonderful things
A bushel of wonderful things
For me to believe in
So world, take me back
I wanna be part of the human race again
And bid good-bye to all my trouble and tears
I've wasted so many odd years
It's time to get even
So world, take me back
I wanna let laughter light up my face again
Oh, no more peekin' through the keyhole
I intend to have my own key
No more sneakin' past the parlor
From now on it's me sittin' on the settee
'Cause today's a day to holler about
For after just sittin' life out
Since heaven knows when
My step has a spring and a drive
I'm suddenly young and alive
You wonderful world take me back again

The world is full of Aprils and Junes
Red roses and yellow balloons
For me to hang on to
So world, take me back
I wanna be part of those good old days again
Whatever happened to those wonderful sights
Those dancing the night away nights
Oh, where have they gone to
So world, take me back
I wanna be there when the gaslights blaze again
Oh, no more watching from the sidelines
I intend to star in the show
No more reaching for tomorrow
From now on I stand with today in my hand
For today the world is ripe as a peach
It's gonna be mine till I reach a hundred and ten
My step has a spring and a drive
I'm suddenly young and alive
You wonderful world take me back again!

▼ Jack Goode and Ethel Merman in the scene preceding "World Take Me Back."

WORLD TAKE ME BACK For one year I had the thrill of hearing the great Merman belt out two songs I had originally written for her. She had turned down originating the role of Dolly but agreed to appear in the show at the end of its run. When I suggested that she sing either "World Take Me Back" or "Before the Parade Passes By," because they basically said the same thing, she responded, "I don't care ... I'll sing 'em both!" — J.H.

LOVE LOOK IN MY WINDOW

Love, look in my window
Love, knock on my door
It's years since you've called on me
How I would love hearing
Your laughter once more
So if you should ever be
In the neighborhood ...
Let's talk about old times
Love, pull up a chair
How I miss your friendly smile
Love, look in my window
Love, knock on my door
Oh, love, come in and stay awhile

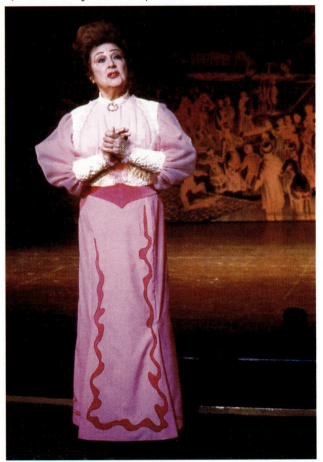

▼ Ethel Merman sings "Love Look in My Window."

JUST LEAVE EVERYTHING TO ME

If you want your sister courted
Brother wed or cheese imported
Just leave ev'rything to me

If you want your roof inspected
Eyebrows tweezed or bill collected
Just leave ev'rything to me

If you want your daughter dated
Or some marriage consummated
For a rather modest fee

If you want a husband spotted
Boyfriend traced or chicken potted
I'll arrange for making all arrangements
Just leave ev'rything to me

If you want your ego bolstered
Muscles toned or chair upholstered
Just leave ev'rything to me

Charming social introductions
Expert mandolin instructions
Just leave ev'rything to me

If you want your culture rounded
French improved or torso pounded
With a ten-year guarantee

If you want a birth recorded
Collies bred or kittens boarded
I'll proceed to plan the whole procedure
Just leave ev'rything to me

If you want a law abolished
Jewelry sold or toenails polished
Just leave everything to me

If you want your liver tested
Glasses made or cash invested
Just leave ev'rything to me

If you want your children coddled
Corsets boned or furs remodeled
Or some nice fresh fricassee
If you want your bustle shifted
Wedding planned or bosom lifted

I'll discreetly use my own discretion
I'll arrange for making all arrangements
I'll proceed to plan the whole procedure
Just leave ev'rything …
To me!

▼Barbra Streisand sings "Just Leave Everything to Me."

JUST LEAVE EVERYTHING TO ME Barbra asked for a new opening number and mentioned that she loved singing "list songs" with lots of complicated lyrics. That's all I had to hear. And, boy, was it wonderfully sung. — J.H.

LOVE IS ONLY LOVE

Don't look for shooting stars
For love is only love
You touch and still you touch the ground
Don't listen for those bells
For love is only love
And if it's love you've found
Your heart won't hear a sound
And when you hold her hand
You only hold her hand
The violins are all a bluff
But if you're really wise
The silence of her eyes
Will tell you
Love is only love
And it's wonderful enough
Without the shooting stars
Without the sound of bells
Without the violins
Love is wonderful enough

▼ Barbra Streisand insists "Love Is Only Love."

▼ *(following pages)* Carol Channing in the "Hello, Dolly!" number.

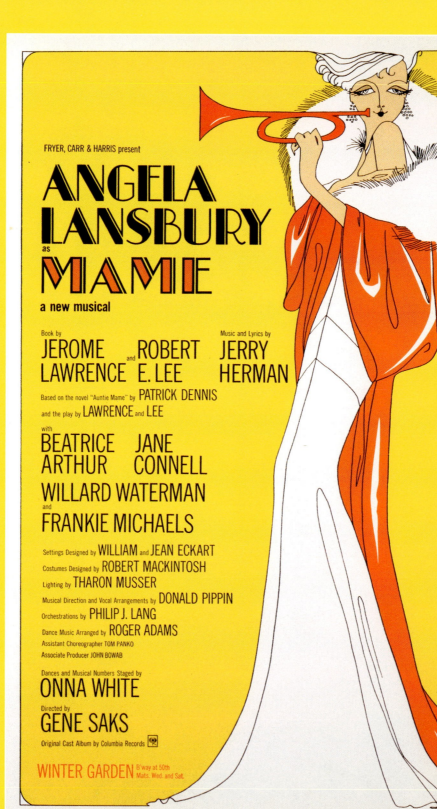

4

MAME

The pressure was on Jerry Herman to provide at least as great a score as *Hello, Dolly!* for his next outing, *Mame.* The show was based on Jerome Lawrence and Robert E. Lee's witty play *Auntie Mame,* which was based on Patrick Dennis's successful novel. The best idea producers Fryer, Carr, and Harris had was hiring Lawrence and Lee to adapt their own play. Their second good idea was casting Angela Lansbury in the lead despite her previous musical outing in the failure, *Anyone Can Whistle.* Director Gene Saks's wife, Beatrice Arthur, was cast in the star-making role of Vera at Jerry's suggestion. Jane Connell as Gooch, Jerry Lanning as Patrick, and Frankie Michaels as Young Patrick completed the leading roles. Onna White, a brilliant, under appreciated choreographer, lent the proceedings a wonderful fluidity, as well as her usual character-driven choreography.

The Winter Garden Theatre on May 24, 1966, was the scene of one of the most exciting openings in Broadway history. *Mame* managed to

MAME

exceed all expectations and became an instant sellout. Angela Lansbury won the Tony Award as did young Frankie Michaels and Beatrice Arthur. *Mame* also was nominated for Tony Awards in the categories of Best Musical, Best Director, Score, Scenic Design (William and Jean Eckart), and Choreography.

Jerry Herman's score was every bit as inspired as his work for *Dolly!*, and he accomplished the miracle of writing two smash-hit title songs in a row. Eydie Gorme had a great success with "If He Walked Into My Life," winning the Grammy Award for Best Female Pop Vocal Performance. And the original cast recording won a Grammy Award for Jerry.

While the number of Mames didn't equal the number of Dollys, the list of actresses who undertook the role is still quite impressive. Janis Paige, Jane Morgan, and Ann Miller completed the Broadway run. Celeste Holm toured the nation, and Susan Hayward played the part of Mame in Las Vegas, Ginger Rogers opened in London (the only woman to play both Dolly and Mame in first-class companies), and in 1974, Lucille Ball was joined by Robert Preston and original Broadway cast members Beatrice Arthur and Jane Connell in the film version of *Mame*. — K.B.

Angela Lansbury advises Frankie Michaels to "Open a New Window." ▶

ST. BRIDGET

Saint Bridget, deliver us to Beekman Place
Away from the wicked and depraved
A gray head is peeping through the curtain lace
Calling "Come ye inside where you'll be saved"

She's baked him a cherry pie and glazed a ham
Her dear arms reach out for his embrace
So if you have pity on this poor lost lamb
God love you dear St. Bridget deliver us to
Bee-e-e-e-e-eekman Place

She'll make up a feather bed our souls to keep
And start every meal by saying grace
So if you have pity on these poor lost sheep
God love you
Dear St. Bridget deliver us to
Bee-e-e-e-e-eekman Place

ST. BRIDGET I began this score with a little hymn expressing what Gooch and Patrick expected to find, which made the contrast of the wild party at Beekman Place even more dynamic. — J.H.

IT'S TODAY An expression my mother used to say when she wanted to celebrate for no particular reason. — J.H.

Jane Connell and Frankie Michaels.

IT'S TODAY

Light the candles
Get the ice out
Roll the rug up
It's today!

Though it may not be anyone's birthday
And though it's far from the first of the year
I know that this very minute
Has history in it, we're here!

It's a time for
Makin' merry
And so I'm for
Makin' hay!
Tune the "grand" up
Dance your shoes off
Strike the band up
It's today!
And we're livin'
And we're well, gang
So raise hell, gang
While we may

Call the cops out
Raise a racket
Pull the stops out
It's today!

Light the candles
Fill the punch bowl
Throw confetti
It's today!
Life can also be lived on a weekday
So don't depend on a holiday date
If you need New Year's to bubble
Then order a double and wait

There's a thank you
You can give life
If you live life
All the way

Pour the scotch out
Hold the roof down
Fellas watch out
It's today!

Tune the "grand" up
Call the cops out
Strike the band up
Pull the stops out
Hallelujah! It's today!

Reprise

Light the sparklers
Crash the cymbals
Blow the bugle
It's today

Someone gave me a wonderful present
Something I needed and yet never knew
So start the whistling and clapping
'Cause under the wrapping was you

And we'll give life
Quite a tumble
And we'll live life
All the way

Call the cops out
Raise a racket
Pull the stops out
It's today!

OPEN A NEW WINDOW

Open a new window
Open a new door
Travel a new highway
That's never been tried before
Before you find you're a dull fellow
Punching the same clock
Walking the same tightrope
As everyone on the block
The fellow you ought to be is three-
    dimensional
Soaking up life down to your toes
Whenever they say you're slightly
    unconventional
Just put your thumb up to your nose
And show 'em how to
Dance to a new rhythm
Whistle a new song
Toast with a new vintage
The fizz doesn't fizz too long
There's only one way to make the bubbles stay
Simply travel a new highway
Dance to a new rhythm
Open a new window ev'ry day

If you follow your Auntie Mame, I'll make
    this vow, my little love
That on the last day of your life
You'll be smiling the same young smile
    you're smiling now, my little love
If you wake up ev'ry morning and you
    pull aside the shutter
And you promise me that these'll be the
    first words that you utter:

Angela Lansbury and Frankie Michaels dance the tango in "Open a New Window."

Open a new window
Open a new door
Travel a new highway
That's never been tried before
Before you find you're a dull fellow
Punching the same clock
Walking the same tightrope
As ev'ryone on the block
The fellow you ought to be is three-
    dimensional
Soaking up life down to your toes
Whenever they say you're slightly
    unconventional
Just put your thumb under your nose
And show 'em how to
Dance to a new rhythm
Whistle a new song
Toast with a new vintage
The fizz doesn't fizz too long
There's only one way to make the bubbles stay
Simply travel a new highway
Dance to a new rhythm
Open a new window ev'ry day

THE MAN IN THE MOON

I have a little secret I'd like to impart
That I hope doesn't give you too much
   of a start
Tho' it's shocking, it's completely true

I know it isn't gossip or rumor, of course
For I have it from quite a reliable source
And I'd like to pass it on to you …

The man in the moon is a lady
A lady with lipstick and curls
The cow that jumped ovah cried "Jumpin'
   Jehovah"
I think it's just one of the girls
She winks at the stars from her bed of
   green cheese
That isn't a nightgown, it's a Saturn chemise, oh
Her friends are the stars and the planets
She sends the Big Dipper a kiss
So don't ever offend 'er, remember her gender
The man in the moon is a miss

▼ Jack Davison (in top hat) listens to Beatrice Arthur's musical astrological lecture, "The Man in the Moon."

MY BEST GIRL

You're my best girl
And nothing you do is wrong
I'm proud you belong to me
And if a day is rough for me
Having you there's enough for me
But if, some day
Another girl comes along
It won't take her long to see
That I'll still be found
Just hangin' around
My best girl

You're my best beau
You're handsome and brave and strong
There's nothing we two can't face
If you're with me, whatever comes
We'll see that trouble never comes
And if someday
Another beau comes along
Determined to take your place
I hope he's resigned
To fall in behind
My best beau

And if someday
When everything turns out wrong
You're through with the human race
Come running to me
For I'll always be
Your best girl

My best girl

Angela Lansbury sings the cut song "Love Is Only Love" to
Frankie Michaels during *Mame's* Boston tryout. Gene Saks asked that
the song and scene be cut to make the show move along faster.
The number would later be used in the film version of *Hello, Dolly!*

WE NEED A LITTLE CHRISTMAS

Haul out the holly
Put up the tree before my spirit falls again!
Fill up the stocking
We may be rushing things but, deck the halls
    again now

For we need a little Christmas
Right this very minute
Candles in the window
Carols at the spinet
Yes, we need a little Christmas
Right this very minute
It hasn't snowed a single flurry
But Santa, dear, we're in a hurry

So climb down the chimney
Turn on the brightest string of lights I've ever
    seen
Slice up the fruitcake
It's time we hung some tinsel on that evergreen
    bough

For I've grown a little leaner, grown a little
    colder
Grown a little sadder, grown a little older
And I need a little angel sitting on my shoulder
Need a little Christmas now!

Haul out the holly
Haven't I taught you well to live each living
    day?
Fill up the stocking

*But, Auntie Mame, it's one week past Thanksgiving
    Day now!*

But we need a little Christmas
Right this very minute
Candles in the window
Carols at the spinet

For we need a little music, need a little laughter
Need a little singing ringing thru the rafter
And we need a little snappy "Happy ever after"
Need a little Christmas now!

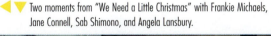

Two moments from "We Need a Little Christmas" with Frankie Michaels, Jane Connell, Sab Shimono, and Angela Lansbury.

THE FOX HUNT

sung in counterpoint

[1]
Look at her go
Look at her fly
Out of the woods
Into the sky
Look how she's bobbin' her head, flappin'
   her feet
She must be glued to the seat!

[2]
Fall off, Auntie Mame, fall off
Fall off, fall off!
Fall off, Auntie Mame, fall off
Before you break your neck!

[3]
She's ruined your bougainvillaea and she's
   smashed your plums
Hell! She's tramplin' your petunias and she's
   mashed your 'mums
But I'm gonna laugh the loudest when the
   judgment comes
For that yella-bellied Yankee

[4]
Giddiyap, Lightnin' Rod
They went west, you go east
Do your stuff, Lightnin' Rod
And giddiyap, giddiyap, you little, dear little
   crazy beast!

Fall off!!

▼ Janis Paige and company.

MAME

You coax the blues right out 'a the horn, Mame
You charm the husk right off 'a the corn, Mame
You've got the banjos strummin'
And plunkin' out a tune to beat the band
The whole plantation's hummin'
Since you brought Dixie back to Dixieland
You make the cotton easy to pick, Mame
You give my old mint julep a kick, Mame
Who ever thought a Yankee would put our little
    Dixie belles to shame?
You've made us feel alive again
You've given us the drive again
To make the South revive again, Mame

You brought the cakewalk back into style,
    Mame
You make the weeping willow tree smile,
    Mame
Your skin is Dixie satin
There's rebel in your manner and your speech
You may be from Manhattan
But Georgia never had a sweeter peach
You make the old magnolia tree bud, Mame
You make camellias bloom in the mud,
    Mame
You make the bougainvillaea turn purple at the
    mention of your name
We're bakin' pecan pies again
Tonight the chicken fries again
This time the South will rise again, Mame

Well, shut my mouth and freeze my face
You've brought some elegance to the place
There's sowbelly, hominy, catfish, and tripe,
    Mame

Well, shut my mouth and damn my eyes
You've made the price of tobacco rise
The old watermelon is suddenly ripe, Mame

And down on the levee a beautiful bevy of
    crinoline ladies has flocked
The way that they're squealin', they give me the
    feelin' the Robert E. Lee must a' docked
The strummin' and ringin', the hummin' and
    singin' is startin' to get out of hand
Since you brought Dixie back to Dixieland

You make our black-eyed peas and our grits,
    Mame
Seem like the bill of fare at the Ritz, Mame
You came, you saw, you conquered and
    absolutely nothing is the same
Your special fascination 'll
Prove to be inspirational
We think you're just sensational
Mame! Mame! Mame!

MAME I didn't want to write another big title song. And I told my producers that lightning doesn't strike twice. Bobby Fryer, one of the producers, came to visit me and practically begged me to try writing one. I was on my way to St. Thomas with Don Pippin, my new musical director, to work on choral arrangements. The combination of Bobby's plea and beautiful tropical weather made my homage to the old South pour out of me on a beach in the Caribbean. Thank you, Bobby. — J.H.

Ginger Rogers at the first day of rehearsal at London's Drury Lane Theatre.

OPENING ACT II

In English lit I'm in the top ten
I've got a B plus average again
Tahiti sounds the greatest of all the crazy places
    that you've been
Wait till you hear the latest: I think I've got a
    whisker on my chin

I find it's getting harder to cram
I flunked my Latin grammar exam
My glands are in a hurry, my voice has sort of
    taken on a roar
The girls I date (don't worry) are socially
    decidedly top drawer

I'm shaving ev'ry morning and growing like
    it's going out of style
The debs all seem to go for me
Give France a big hello for me
A hug to Uncle Beau for me

(Spoken) Your loving nephew, Patrick

▲ Frankie Michaels and Jerry Lanning in the Act II reprise of "Mame."

▲ *(previous pages)* Charles Brasswell, Angela Lansbury, and Frankie Michaels as the curtain falls on Act I.

BOSOM BUDDIES Angie and Bea, God bless them, stopped the show nightly with this song. — J.H.

BOSOM BUDDIES

We'll always be bosom buddies
Friends, sisters, and pals
We'll always be bosom buddies
If life should reject you, there's me to protect you
If I say that your tongue is vicious
If I call you uncouth
It's simply that who else but a bosom buddy
Will sit down and tell you the truth?

Though now and again I'm aware that my
    candid opinion may sting
Tho' often my frank observation might scald
I've been meaning to tell you for years you
    should keep your hair nat'ral like mine

If I kept my hair nat'ral like yours, I'd be bald!
But, darling

We'll always be dear companions
My crony
My mate
We'll always be harmonizing
Orphan Annie and Sandy
Like Amos and Andy
If I say that your sense of style's as far off as
    your youth: It's only that
Who else but a bosom buddy will tell you the
    whole stinkin' truth?

Each time that a critic has written "Your voice
    is the voice of a frog"
Straight to your side to defend you I rush
You know that I'm there ev'ry time that the
    world makes an unkind remark
When they say: "Vera Charles is the world's
    greatest lush"

It hurts me

And if I say your fangs are showing; Mame,
    pull in your claws
It's simply that who else but a bosom buddy
    would notice the obvious flaws

I feel it's my duty to tell you it's time to adjust
    to your age
You try to be "Peg o' My Heart" when you're
    Lady Macbeth!
Exactly how old are you, Vera? The truth!

Well, how old do you think?

I'd say somewhere between forty and death!

But sweetie

I'll always be Alice Toklas
If you'll be Gertrude Stein
And tho' I'll admit I've dished you
I've gossiped and gloated, but I'm so devoted
And if I say that sex and guts made you into
    a star
Remember that who else but a bosom buddy
    will tell you how rotten you are
Just turn to your bosom buddy
For aid and affection, for help and direction
For loyalty, love, and forsooth
Remember that
Who else but a bosom buddy
Will sit down and level and give you the devil
Will sit down and tell you the truth!

Angela Lansbury and Beatrice Arthur do the "son-of-a bitch step"
(as Bea Arthur referred to it) in "Bosom Buddies."

GOOCH'S SONG

With my wings resolutely spread, Missus
    Burnside
And my old inhibitions shed, Missus Burnside
I did each little thing you said, Missus Burnside
I lived! I lived! I lived!

I altered the drape of a drop of my bodice
And softened the shape of my brow
I followed directions and made some
    connections
But what do I do now?

Who'd think this Miss Prim would have opened
    a window
As far as her whim would allow?
And who would suppose it was so hard to
    close it
Oh, what do I do now?

I polished and powdered and puffed myself
If life is a banquet I stuffed myself

I had my misgivings but went on a field trip
To find out what living's about
My thanks for the training: now I'm not
    complaining
But you left something out!

Instead of wand'ring on with my lone remorse
I have come back home to complete the course
Oh, what do I do …

I traveled to hell in my new veneer
And look what I got as a souvenir!

But still I'll defend you as guide and instructor
Would I recommend you? And how!
Although I was leery, I thrived on your theory
That life can be a wow!
And so I wandered on till I found my prince
And have I been nauseous ever since
Oh, what do I do now?

Angela Lansbury (in one of her many wigs eliminated during the Philadelphia out-of-town engagement) arriving at the Upson's barbecue prior to "That's How Young I Feel." She originally wore a succession of wigs throughout the show but didn't have time to change into them so her own haircut was retained for the entire show.

THAT'S HOW YOUNG I FEEL

I have the feeling that time has halted
I'd like two straws and a choc'late malted
'Cause that's how young I feel

I feel like "peckin" and "bunny-huggin"
And "lindy-hoppin" and "jitter-buggin"
'Cause that's how young I feel

I'm mad for that big band beat
Wanna ride in a rumble seat
(Sheldon's got the Chevy)

Love a face full of frozen custard
To have a hot dog with sand and mustard
And ride the Ferris wheel
Oh, honey, 'cause that's how young I feel

I'm ready to ask my mom
Can I go to the Junior Prom?
(Sheldon's got the Chevy)

Love a "coonskin" to knock about with
To start each morning by giving out with
A Rudy Vallee squeal!
Oh, honey, 'cause that's how young I feel

Love a face full of frozen custard
To have a hot dog with sand and mustard
And ride the Ferris wheel
Oh, honey, 'cause that's how young I feel
Young I feel! Young I feel!

▼ Angela Lansbury shows the chorus a thing or two in "That's How Young I Feel."

IF HE WALKED INTO MY LIFE

Where's that boy with the bugle
My little love who was always my big romance
Where's that boy with the bugle
And why did I ever buy him those damn long
    pants

Did he need a stronger hand
Did he need a lighter touch
Was I soft or was I tough
Did I give enough? Did I give too much
At the moment that he needed me
Did I ever turn away
Would I be there when he called
If he walked into my life today

Were his days a little dull
Were his nights a little wild
Did I overstate my plan?
Did I stress the man and forget the child
And there must have been a million things
That my heart forgot to say
Would I think of one or two
If he walked into my life today

Should I blame the times I pampered him or
    blame the times I bossed him
What a shame I never really found the boy
    before I lost him

Were the years a little fast
Was his world a little free
Was there too much of a crowd
All too lush and loud and not enough of me
Tho' I'll ask myself my whole life long
What went wrong along the way
Would I make the same mistakes
If he walked into my life today

If that boy with the bugle
Walked into my life today

▼ Angela Lansbury sings "If He Walked Into My Life." Although the
same scene as that of "That's How Young I Feel" notice that Angela is
wearing three different dresses.

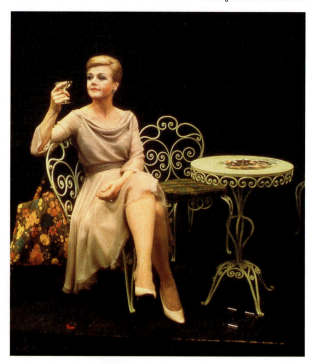

IF HE WALKED INTO MY LIFE In the
middle of writing the score, I realized that neither the novel nor the Lawrence
and Lee play had addressed the heartbreaking moment of discovering
that the person whose life you most influenced has turned into a symbol
of everything you've always fought against. For me, Angela Lansbury's
delivery of this song was the strongest moment in *Mame*. — J.H.

IT'S TODAY - REPRISE

Pickled python
Peppered sheep spleen
Have some owl eggs
It's today

I said: Ito, do something exotic
Just try a little bit harder to please
And he's been extra ambitious, try these:
    they're delicious
They're bees!

And we're livin' and we're well, gang
So, raise hell, gang
While we may
Call the cops out
Raise a racket
Pull the stops out
It's today

Mame throws a party for the Upsons. ▶
Back row: Sab Shimono, Diana Walker, Jerry Lanning, and
Diane Coupe (on ladder). Front row: Johanna Douglas,
Angela Lansbury, John C. Becher, and Willard Waterman.

LOVING YOU

Loving you is snow and jasmine
And the noise of New Year's Eve
Loving you is now and yesterday
Is real and make believe
Loving you is Rome and New Orleans
And gazing at the lazy summer skies
Fireworks reflecting in your eyes
Foolish and improbable and wise
And loving you is tart as lemonade and sweet
    as April wine
Loving you is watching all the lovely things
    of life combine
In your arms, I'm all I wish I were
I'm brave, I'm strong, and I'm true
As long as I can go on living, loving you

LOVING YOU Written for Robert Preston for the unfortunate film of *Mame* — J.H.

▼ Lucille Ball and Robert Preston in the film version.

▼ (*Mames, following pages*) **1** Angela Lansbury.
2 Susan Hayward. **3** Ann Miller.
4 Celeste Holm. **5** Ginger Rogers.

ANGELA LANSBURY
DEAR WORLD

5

DEAR WORLD

Dear World was based on Maurice Valency's *The Madwoman of Chaillot*, an adaptation of Jean Giraudoux's play *La Folle de Chaillot*, a special favorite of Jerry's ever since he played the Deaf-Mute in a production at the University of Miami.

Jerry Herman knew *Dear World* would be a difficult undertaking. Still, he and the rest of the production team felt that a career must include risks and the stretching of creative muscles. Jerry and producer Alexander Cohen assembled many members of the *Mame* company: Angela Lansbury, Lawrence and Lee, Jane Connell, orchestrator extraordinaire Philip J. Lang, and conductor Donald Pippin. Although they knew the adaptation would be challenging, they couldn't have imagined just how many troubles the production would endure.

Changes in the creative staff (three directors and two choreographers) during the out-of-town tryouts haunted the production. The necessity

DEAR WORLD

of the adjective "big" to go with the words "Broadway musical" doomed what might have been a charming chamber musical and turned *Dear World* into a stylish but overblown evening. When the show finally opened on February 6, 1969, after almost two months of previews, there was faint praise for the piece itself although Lansbury's performance was universally applauded. She won her second Tony Award and Oliver Smith's scenic designs were also nominated.

The pain of the poor reception accorded *Dear World* was somewhat offset by the continuing success of *Hello, Dolly!* and *Mame*. But the seriousness and experimentation of the score for *Dear World* threw critics off balance. They somehow expected another razzle-dazzle musical-comedy score even though the source material demanded an intelligent, sensitive musical-theatre approach. Luckily, there can be second chances for shows. Jerry, along with his collaborators Lawrence and Lee, reworked the libretto and score and simplified the proceedings. Recent revivals of *Dear World* at the Sundance Festival and the Goodspeed Opera House with small, intimate productions have shown the strength and charms of *Dear World*. — K.B.

▲▲▲▲▲▲▲▲▲▲▲▲▲▲▲▲▲▲▲▲▲▲▲▲▲▲▲▲▲▲▲▲▲▲▲▲

Angela Lansbury. ▶

A SENSIBLE WOMAN

A sensible woman will walk through the sewers
To keep her hat out of the rain
A sensible woman will not bother her poor
    head at night
With thoughts of thieves that prowl about
She wears her pearls to bed at night
A sensible woman grows spirited flowers
By watering them with champagne
And even when life may seem
Distraught with inhumanity
Reason and rhyme and sanity gone
With her head on her shoulders
Her hand on her hat pin
A sensible woman goes on

A sensible woman creates her own fashion
Believing that hats should be <u>hats</u>
She writes herself letters filled
With witty past and present news
That way she's sure tomorrow that
The news she gets is pleasant news
A sensible woman when faced with a problem
Confers with her sensible cats
And even when face to face
With all the world's banality
Its individuality gone
With her eye on its target
Her parasol brandished
A sensible woman goes on

A sensible woman will trade with the grocer
Some gossip for onions and rice
And then when her birthday comes
She'll simply say "away with it"
She'll add another beauty spot
She'll choose an age and stay with it
A sensible woman sets traps for the landlord
And plays with the neighborhood mice
And if there's a moment when

The night seems dark and endless and
Her life seems pale and friendless and wan
With a grasp of her senses
A grip on her handbag
With wisdom and wit and elan
With courage and cat food
With grit and galoshes
A sensible woman goes on
And on
And on
And on
And on!

A SENSIBLE WOMAN Cut in Boston, returned
to the score permanently at Goodspeed and Sundance. — J.H.

THE SPRING OF NEXT YEAR

There will be a sweet taste in the air
From industrial waste in the air
And your eyelids will smart from the sting of
The smog in the Spring of
Next year

There will be a black slick on the Seine
And the sludge will be thick on the Seine
And your eardrums will thrill to the ring of
The ax in the Spring of
Next year

Ahh, the apple trees blooming
As they're crushed into pulp
There'll be smoke stacks consuming
Each available gulp
That's inhalable

But the moment most thrilling begins
When the pneumatic drilling begins
It's a song that all Paris will sing
In the bountiful Spring of
Next year

We'll be watching the statues corrode
We'll be hearing the fountains explode
It's a song that the hatchets will ring
And the derricks will swing
And all Paris will sing
In the bountiful Spring of
Next year

Left to right: Alexander Cohen, Lucia Victor (the original director), Angela Lansbury, Jerome Lawrence, Robert E. Lee, and Jerry Herman at the piano.

TOMORROW MORNING

If your world falls flat on its face today
You can erase today
Tomorrow morning
You'll discover all of your past mistakes
Gone when the world awakes
Tomorrow morning
You will see your life in a different light
Crystal and crisp and clear
And quite
Worth beginning over
There's no long lost star that you cannot reach
For your perfect day starts each
Tomorrow morning
You're brave
Tomorrow morning
You're strong
Tomorrow morning
You can begin again!

You'll wake up the luckiest man on earth
Proud that your little life
Is worth
Going on forever
There's no long lost star that you cannot reach
For your perfect day starts each
Tomorrow morning
You're brave
Tomorrow morning
You're strong
Tomorrow morning
You can begin again!

◀ Angela Lansbury and Kurt Peterson.

I DON'T WANT TO KNOW

If music is no longer lovely
If laughter is no longer lilting
If lovers are no longer loving
Then I don't want to know

If summer is no longer carefree
If children are no longer singing
If people are no longer happy
Then I don't want to know

Let me hide every truth from my eyes
With the back of my hand
Let me live in a world full of lies
With my head in the sand

For my memories all are exciting
My memories all are enchanted
My memories burn in my head with a
    steady glow
So if, my friends, if love is dead
I don't want to know

I DON'T WANT TO KNOW Another hotel-room song … I would go several times a week to stand in the back of the Mark Hellinger Theatre and watch Angela Lansbury stop the show with this song. — J.H.

▼ Angela Lansbury and Pamela Hall.

Angela Lansbury. ▶

I'VE NEVER SAID I LOVE YOU

I've walked in the dawn
On somebody's arm
And looked at the lights along the shore
But I've never said "I love you"
So when I say "I love you"
He'll know I've never loved before

I've touched in the dark
And laughed in the rain
And listened to all the old clichés
But I've never said "I love you"
I'm saving my "I love you"
For someone worthy of the phrase
For somebody wise and strong and tall
And yet, he may not be that at all

I only know
We'll turn and we'll look
We'll nod and we'll know
We'll stare and we'll smile
And then, and then
I'll gratefully say "I love you"
And when I say "I love you"
He'll know I've never loved before
He'll know I'll never love again

(spoken) I love you!

I'll gratefully say "I love you"
And when I say "I love you"
He'll know I've never loved before
He'll know I'll never love again

◀ Pamela Hall.

GARBAGE

Pâté de foie gras
Thursday's gardenias
Ribbon and orange rinds
A volume of Chaucer
Bound in Morocco
Lilies and coffee grinds
The pit of a peach
The stem of a cherry
Floating in pink champagne
There was a time when garbage was a pleasure
When you found the sound of good and plenty
Gurgling in your drain

The world was all ginger and lime
The world was the rustle of silk
Purple and puce
Crystal and lace
Fresh orange juice
Ginger and lime

The shell of a clam
The claw of a lobster
Hairpins and chocolate mousse
A page of *Othello*
Gilt at the edges
Daisies and charlotte russe
A rose and a fan
A piece of pimento
Floating in turquoise ink
There was a time when garbage was a pleasure
When you found the joy of gracious living
Underneath your sink

The world was all nutmeg and thyme
The world was a Viennese waltz
Played with a lilt
Velvet and bronze
Silver and gilt
Nutmeg and thyme!

A raspberry tart
A hint of meringue
A vision in rose and white
A fragment of lace
A sliver of crystal
Catching the morning light
A glimpse of an old engraved invitation
Makes one take pause and think
About the time when garbage was a pleasure
When you found the joy of gracious living
Underneath your sink

There was a time when garbage was a pleasure
When you found the joy of gracious living
Underneath your sink

▼ Angela Lansbury and Milo O'Shea.

Milo O'Shea, Angela Lansbury, Carmen Mathews, and Jane Connell in "Garbage." ▶

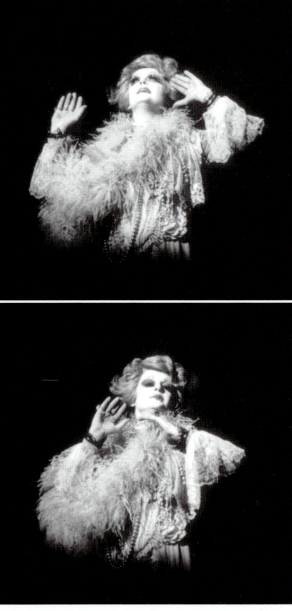

▲ Angela Lansbury sings "I Don't Want to Know."

DEAR WORLD

Someone has wounded you, dear world
Someone has poisoned you, dear world
And those who love you defiantly insist
That you get off the critical list
So make your recovery quick, world
We're sick of having a sick world
We want you dancing tomorrow afternoon
So be a dear world, and get well soon

Please take your medicine, dear world
Please make the fever break, dear world
Your vim and vigor are very sorely missed
Help us declare you "patient dismissed"
And stand on your crutches with pride, world
You've gotta save your own hide, world
We're not quite ready to trade you for the moon
So be a dear world, and get well soon

Someone has beaten you, dear world
Someone has blinded you, dear world
Make sure your heartbeat is very finely tuned
Take off the bandage
Heal every wound
And let's show the whole human race, world
You're not a terminal case, world
We're not quite ready to trade you for the moon
So be a dear world, and get well soon

They won't defeat you, world
This we assure you, world
If we can treat you, world
Then we can cure you, world

Someone has wounded you, dear world
Someone has poisoned you, dear world
And those who love you defiantly insist
That you get off the critical list
And let's show the whole human race, world
You're not a terminal case, world
We're not quite ready to trade you for the moon
So be a dear world, and get well soon

▲ The marquee of the Mark Hellinger Theatre.

DEAR WORLD This is one of the only songs I've ever written that I wish I hadn't. — J.H.

KISS HER NOW

Before you half remember what her smile
    was like
Before you half recall the day you found her
Kiss her now
While she's young
Kiss her now
While she's yours
Kiss her now
While she needs your arms around her
For if you let a moment come between
    you now
It soon becomes a day, a year, a lifetime
Blink your eye
Turn your head
And you've lost her
And you'll spend half your life wond'ring how
So before you forget how you loved her
Kiss her now
Kiss her now
Kiss her now!

Blink your eye
Turn your head
And you've lost her
And you'll spend half your life wond'ring how
So before you forget how you loved her
Kiss her now
Kiss her now
Kiss her now!

Angela Lansbury. ▶

THE TEA PARTY

MEMORIES

I remember Claude
His face was gaunt; his skin was pale
His bony little fingers were so delicate and frail
Yes, I remember Claude in every intimate
  detail
But I remember absolutely nothing
About my husband

And I remember Georges
His voice was deep and insincere
His hot and heavy breathing and his lewd
  licentious leer
The passionate obscenities he whispered in
  my ear
But I remember absolutely nothing
About my husband

PEARLS

Suppose I were to say your pearls were false

They were. They were.

Everybody knows when you wear pearls
That little by little the pearls become real

And isn't it the same with memories?

DICKIE

Dickie
Darling little Dickie
I'm so proud of my little, plump little, shy
  little cuddly chap
Dickie
(kiss … kiss … kiss … kiss …)
Dickie
Always lying flat on your fat tummy
Here in your dear mummy's lap
Stop barking
Even
When I have to scold you
Mummy's just as thrilled as can be
How magnificently you obey

(spoken) He's an absolute monster.

I will not sit back and allow you to insult
  him this way
Dickie
Poor Dickie
Dear Dickie
The fact is, my dears, that I didn't even
  bring him today!

THE TEA PARTY I feel that I got closest to truly
musicalizing Giraudoux with this mad triple counterpoint chattering of
three madwomen. Walter Kerr called it "close to light opera and close
to perfection." — J.H.

Jane Connell sings of Dickie. ▶

VOICES
Chatter, chatter, chatter
There are voices in my pantry
That are wishing me a hearty appetite
Gurgle, gurgle, gurgle
There are voices in my teapot
With advice for housewives

Chatter, chatter, chatter
There are voices in my pillow
That have come to tuck me in and spend
    the night
And voices in my vacuum cleaner
That can be extremely impolite

Chatter, chatter, chatter
There are voices in my closet
Saying "Wear the fuchsia gloves and purple
    veil"
And voices in my piano singing up and down
    the oriental scale
If I welcome them and take them to my bosom
It's quite obvious indeed
That those lovely little voices are the only
    friends a girl will ever need

THOUGHTS
Everything that was ... is
Everything that lived ... lives
Every little thought ever thought is as
    lasting as time
Everything that was ... is
Everything that is ... will be
Some distant day they'll be saying the saying
    that I'm saying now
For we are not alone ... here
There are other minds ... here
Moliere and Keats are enraged and engaged
    in a row
Listen to the lovely language
Every lesson Voltaire ever taught
And every thought that Buddha ever thought
Are right here
In this air
In this house
In this room with us now

Carmen Mathews hears the "Voices" in her hot water bottle. ▶

▼ *(following pages)* The three madwomen of Paris gather for a "Tea Party."

AND I WAS BEAUTIFUL

He stood and looked at me
And I was beautiful
For it was beautiful
How he believed in me
His love was strong enough
To make me anything
So I was everything
He wanted me to be
But then he walked away
And took my smile with him
And now the years blur by
But every now and then
I stop and think of him
And how he looked at me
And all at once
I'm beautiful again

For a moment …
I'm beautiful again

AND I WAS BEAUTIFUL My idol, Irving Berlin, unknowingly taught me that less is more — J.H.

Angela Lansbury. ▶

Kurt Peterson and Angela Lansbury. ▶

HAVE A LITTLE PITY ON THE RICH

If I throw a diamond in the Seine
It comes up in the trout I have for dinner
If I bet a bundle on a mare with rickets
Well, the mare becomes a winner
If I throw a franc away
Or give a bank away
Or drop my assets in a ditch
The more that it's money to burn to me
The faster the profits return to me
So have a little pity on the rich

If I'm bent at losing at roulette
I break the bank at every single sitting
If I buy a shabby little stock in April
Well, by May the damn thing's splitting
With my fortune flaunting me
My holdings haunting me
My coupons clipped at fever pitch
My capital gains are constricting me
My wealth is a plague that's afflicting me
So have a little pity on the rich

O, Lord, make me ragged at the seams
Lord, turn my caviar to hash
I want my pocket full of dreams
Instead of filthy rotten cash
So pity me, pity me, pity me

How I'd love to be the simple slob
Who has to sweat to earn his bread and butter
How I long to be the blissful bum
Who knows the joy of starving in the gutter
With my cash provoking me
My blue chips choking me
I swear, your honor, it's a bitch
I think of how calm and secure I was
When decent and honest and poor I was
Oh, I'd prefer it vastly
Slaving for my supper
It's absolutely ghastly
Being upper upper
So have a little pity on the rich

My capital gains are constricting me
My wealth is a plague that's afflicting me
Oh, life was spare but sunny
Life was bare but free, friends
I don't worship money
Money worships me, friends
So have a little pity on the rich!

An out-of-town picture of Michael Kermoyan (center).
His part was cut prior to New York.

THROUGH THE BOTTOM OF THE GLASS

What a fascinating view
Through the bottom of the glass
A December afternoon looks particularly well
When you watch it drift along
Through some sunny muscatel
It's the middle of July
Through the bottom of the glass

What a fascinating view
Through the facets in the ice
The beggars and the rogues
That we socially condemn
Are the court of Antoinette
Through the prism of the stem
So I watch them saunter by
Through the bottom of the glass

In the cold clear light of afternoon
You see the cobwebs and the patches and
the tears
In the cold clear light of afternoon
You count the wrinkles and the mem'ries
and the years

But there's humor and there's youth
Through the garnet of the port
And the hussy from Marseilles
Who's a common little drear
Has a rather regal air
Through the topaz of the beer
She's a cultured little lass
Through a sip of anisette
Through the crystal of the gin
Through a layer of chartreuse
Through the bottom of the glass

▲ Angela Lansbury and the cast singing "Through the Bottom of the Glass."

In the brazen blazing of the sun
You feel the pressure and the tension and
the hurt
In the brazen blazing of the sun
You see the gossip and the hunger and the dirt

But there's majesty and truth
In a tall aperitif
When a crisis in the world
Rips my countrymen in half
Through the bubbles of champagne
They invariably laugh
So I simply let life pass
Through the rose of the rosé
Through the amber of the rum
Through an endless pousse-café
Through the bottom of the glass

THROUGH THE BOTTOM OF THE GLASS Also cut in Boston . . . I felt it was too static. — J.H.

JUST A LITTLE BIT MORE

There's always room for just a
 little bit more
There's always room for just a
 little bit more
Most people fail to see the
 infinite scope and the
 endless extent
Of their capacity
And so when I have licked the
 plate clean
When I have picked the bones
 and passed the last bean
When I am stuffed and gorged
 and glutted and bloated
I still hunger for
Just a mite of a mousse
Just a gram of Gruyère
Just a teeny soufflé
Just a tiny éclair
Just a little bit more
Just a little bit more

There's always room for just a
 little bit more
Go on and force yourself a
 little bit more
Most people never know how
 high and how wide and
 how totally vast
Their own potential is
So when they print my name
 on the door
And when I'm managing the
 whole seventh floor
And when they finally go and
 make me the President

Think what's in store
I can hardly keep up
With my changing facade
In a month I'll be King
In a year I'll be God
Just a little bit more
Just a little bit more

There's always room for just a
 little bit more
Go on, enjoy yourself just a
 little bit more
Most people fail to see the
 towering height and the
 staggering depth
Of their capacity
So Monday night I sleep Kiki
And Tuesday night Paulette,
 and Wednesday Marie
And Thursday morning Claire,
 Friday my muscles
Are weary and sore
But I'm willing to try some
 unusual sins
A Mongolian tart
Or some Siamese twins
Just a little bit more
Just a little bit more

Taking francs from the rich
Has a certain allure
But it's even more fun
When you're screwing the
 poor
Just a little bit more
Just a little bit more

For each man has a natural
 desire
To find a plot of earth that he
 can acquire
And so to rest my bones the
 day I retire
I would simply adore
Just an acre of ground
One respectable piece
Just a little backyard
Argentina or Greece
Just a little bit more
Just a little bit more

And so when we have licked
 the plate clean
When we have picked the
 bones and passed the last
 bean
When we are stuffed and
 gorged and glutted and
 bloated
We still hunger for
Just a mite of a mousse
Just a gram of Gruyère
Just a teeny soufflé
Just a tiny éclair
Just a little bit more
Just a little bit more

ONE PERSON

One person can beat a drum
And make enough noise for ten
One person can blow a horn
And that little boom and that little blare
Can make a hundred others care
And one person can hold a torch
And light up the sky again
And one little voice that's squeaking a song
Can make a million voices strong
If one person can beat a drum
And one person can blow a horn
If one person can hold a torch
Then one person can change the world

There may be an army of them
And only a handful of us
And how can a poor little band
Fight a mighty regime?

There may be a legion of them
And only a parcel of us
But it isn't the size of the fist
It's the size of the dream

One person can beat a drum
And make enough noise for ten
One person can blow a horn
And that little boom and that little blare
Can make a hundred others care
One person can hold a torch
And light up the sky again
And one little voice that's squeaking a song
Can make a million voices strong
If one person can beat a drum
And one person can blow a horn
If one person can hold a torch
Then one person can change the world!

6

MACK AND MABEL

The saddest failure of Jerry Herman's career is *Mack and Mabel*. The show appeared to have all the right elements: box-office names Bernadette Peters and Robert Preston, genius director/choreographer Gower Champion, and ace librettist Michael Stewart. But it was another victim of its time, an era when rock musicals were preferred over traditional musical comedy scores. Deep at its core was a simple love story and an exceptionally appropriate score. The urge to turn what could have been a bittersweet musical drama into a huge musical comedy was fatal to *Mack and Mabel*.

For his part, Jerry Herman created what many consider to be his finest score. Delicately avoiding bathos, the character songs are beautifully romantic with more than a tinge of regret and, continuing in the maturity evinced in *Dear World,* a touch of cynicism. Despite Jerry Herman's reputation as a writer of strong women's roles, Mack has as important a singing part as Mabel.

MACK AND MABEL

The show itself divided the critics at its opening on October 6, 1974, receiving both raves and pans. But word-of-mouth was strong and the show was beginning to build its audience. The original cast recording helped bolster the box-office, but its theatre owners lost patience with the slowly building ticket sales. The show closed after only 66 performances.

As the years since the show's opening have passed, *Mack and Mabel* has gained an almost legendary caché. Its songs have been adopted by many singers with "I Won't Send Roses" becoming a modern standard. As the score became more and more known, demand for a new production grew. Both Jerry and librettist Michael Stewart began reworking the show for a future production. Unfortunately, Michael Stewart's death brought that work to a close and future revised productions of the show were postponed.

Now, *Mack and Mabel* has been retooled putting an emphasis on its core story, the love affair between Mack Sennett and Mabel Normand. Francine Pascal, sister of Michael Stewart, has worked with Jerry on clarifying and strengthening the book. A reading of the new piece, held before the public in Los Angeles, was an unqualified success. Jerry's score shines through in this new version giving its emotional palette even more richness. A new Broadway mounting of a streamlined *Mack and Mabel* is eagerly awaited by the show's many supporters. — K.B.

Stanley Simmonds welcomes Bernadette Peters's Mabel back to the studio.

MOVIES WERE MOVIES

Movies were movies when you paid a dime
    to escape
Cheering the hero and hissing the man in
    the cape
Romance and action and thrills
"Pardner there's gold in them hills"
Movies were movies when during the titles
    you'd know
You'd get a happy ending
Dozens of blundering cops in a thundering
    chase
Getting a bang out of lemon meringue in
    the face
Bandits attacking a train
One little tramp with a cane
Movies were movies were movies when I ran
    the show

Movies were movies when Pauline was tied to
    the track
After she trudged through the ice with a babe
    on her back
Girls at the seashore would stand
All in a row in the sand
Rolling their stockings an inch and a quarter
    below
The line of decency
Swanson and Keaton and Dressler and William
    S. Hart
No one pretended that what we were doing
    was art
We had some guts and some luck
But we were just makin' a buck
Movies were movies were movies when I ran
    the show!

MOVIES WERE MOVIES is a strong number because in it Mack is defying the new Hollywood: the talkies. It shows him intractable, tough and proud. — J.H.

Robert Preston as Mack Sennett sings "Movies Were Movies." ▶

▲ Jerry Dodge, Bernadette Peters, Robert Fitch, and cast singing "Look What Happened to Mabel."

LOOK WHAT HAPPENED TO MABEL All the songs in the show are totally different in style, and together they make the score into a bouquet of mixed colors, that I think is my best work. I've always been disappointed that *Mack and Mabel* never found its true place. But I think there's a still a chance for it. There'll be a new production starting in Houston later this year that will tour around the country. — J.H.

LOOK WHAT HAPPENED TO MABEL

Miss waitress from Flatbush get down from
  up there
Don't you know that you're out of your class
Miss waitress from Flatbush I hope you're
  aware
You're behaving like some little ass
Hey miss
What's this …

See that fascinating creature
With perfection stamped on every feature
She was plain little Nellie
The kid from the deli
But mother of God look what happened
  to Mabel

From now on this pile of flesh'll
Be considered somethin' pretty special
And Miss B.L.T. down
Is the toast of the town
Mary and Joseph … what happened to Mabel

Every gesture and position that she takes
Is smart and meticulous
Talk about the magic that the camera makes
But this is ridiculous …

Hold your tongue and hold your snickers
For the new enchantress of the flickers
Is that plain little Nellie
The kid from the deli
So rattle me beads
Look what happened to Mabel!

Someone who was plain as mutton
On the screen is cuter than a button
And the girl with the pickles
Who hustled for nickels
Is somethin' to see. … Look what happened
  to Mabel

Yesterday a tip collector
But today just turn on that projector
And Miss Avenoo R
Is a regular star
Mother Machree look what happened to Mabel

Up to now I never really knew that I
Could be so ambitious
But suddenly I know I have to say goodbye
To bagels and knishes
O, St. Aloysius
I know that you might think I'm balmy
But the queen of corned beef and salami
Is that glamorous goddess
Who's bustin' her bodice
Oh, jumpin' St. Jude …
Look what happened to Ma-a-a-bel!

BIG TIME

This time it's the big time
In a short time we can be
The cherry on the top of the sundae
The shiny star on top of the tree
So you'd better
Grab it with your both hands
When that great moment arrives
'Cause this time it's the big time
It's the big time of our lives

This time it's the extra
It's the special, it's the plus
This time we won't say "Those lucky bastards"
This time those lucky bastards are us
Ain't we somethin'!
Farewell to the small time
To the fleabags and the dives
'Cause this time it's the big time
It's the big time of our lives!

I'm gonna buy myself a Pierce-Arrow
And wave to all my fans in the streets
I'm gonna have a mansion like Pickford's
I'm gonna sleep on black satin sheets

And we'll raise more hell, make more hay
Than decent fellas should
Because the gang from King's Highway
Is going Hollywood!

This time it's the big time
And it's high time we were seen
By ev'ry dapper dude in Dakota
On ev'ry scroungy neighborhood screen
So you'd better

Grab it with your both hands
When that great moment arrives
'Cause this time it's the big time
It's the big time of our lives!

This time it's the extra
It's the special, it's the plus
This time we won't say "Those lucky bastards"
This time those lucky bastards are us
Ain't we somethin'!
In each hundred million
There's a handful that survives
And this time we're that handful
So it's bye-bye to the small time
This time and for all time
It's the big big big time of our lives!

Robert Preston and Lisa Kirk at the beginning of "Big Time." ▶

▲ Jerry Dodge, Nancy Evers, Bernadette Peters, Robert Fitch, Robert Preston, Lisa Kirk, Tom Batten, Christopher Murney, and Bert Michaels sing "Big Time."

Robert Preston and Bernadette Peters in "I Won't Send Roses."

I WON'T SEND ROSES Probably my most interesting ballad. I knew I had to write a song about a man who couldn't say "I love you." But I knew it still had to be a romantic song. Aware that I didn't know how to accomplish this, I wrote the entire score and kept avoiding this scene.

I used to write a lot of my lyrics walking around New York City. I would often find myself a mile away from my home putting rhymes together. One day I passed a little florist shop. It was early spring and they had put out dozens and dozens of bunches of roses on the sidewalk. The flowers were all glistening in the sun. ... It was a beautiful, romantic sight. I instantly wrote, "I won't send roses or hold the door," and got the idea of using all the reasons Mabel shouldn't have anything to do with Mack. I jumped to the last line and knew I had the makings of a distinctive song; a warning by a man who cares enough to caution the person he loves. — J.H.

I WON'T SEND ROSES

I won't send roses
Or hold the door
I won't remember
Which dress you wore
My heart is too much in control
The lack of romance in my soul
Will turn you gray, kid
So stay away, kid
Forget my shoulder
When you're in need
Forgetting birthdays
Is guaranteed
And should I love you, you would be
The last to know
I won't send roses
And roses suit you so ...

My pace is frantic
My temper's cross
With words romantic
I'm at a loss
I'd be the first one to agree
That I'm preoccupied with me
And it's inbred, kid
So keep your head, kid
In me you'll find things
Like guts and nerve
But not the kind things
That you deserve
And so while there's a fighting chance
Just turn and go
I won't send roses
And roses suit you so

Reprise

So who needs roses
Or stuff like that
So who wants chocolates
They'd make me fat
And I can get along just fine
Without a gushing valentine
And I'll get by, kid
With just the guy, kid
And if he calls me
And it's collect
Sir Walter Raleigh
I don't expect
And though I know I may be left
Out on a limb
So who needs roses
That didn't come from him

Bernadette Peters sings the reprise of "I Won't Send Roses." ▶

I WANNA MAKE THE WORLD LAUGH

Heartbreak and passion
May both be in fashion
But I wanna make the world laugh
Let others do drama of sin and disgrace
While I throw a fish in the heroine's face
To keep them in stitches
I'd burn the star's britches
And saw Cousin Sally in half
Let Mr. Griffith deal with humanity's woes
I'd rather film the guy with the fly on his nose
My goal and my mission
My burning ambition
Is . . . I wanna make the world laugh!

Some have a leaning
For dark hidden meaning
But I wanna make the world laugh
Let other directors film tragic romance
But I like a hero with ants in his pants
Nothing I've found is
As sweet as that sound is
The music that fattens the calf
My great new plot is not about tyranny's lash
It deals with itching powder and papa's
    mustache
This curse I've been blessed with
Completely possessed with
Is . . . I wanna make the world laugh!

Nothing I've found is
As sweet as that sound is
The music that fattens the calf
So keep the suds, the schmaltz, and the soap
    and the sobs
The only art I know is to tickle the slobs
This curse I've been blessed with
Completely possessed with
Is . . . I wanna make the world laugh!

▼ Robert Preston sings "I Wanna Make the World Laugh."

▶▼ "I Wanna Make the World Laugh."

MACK AND MABEL

As a pair there's nothin' greata'
Than this cupcake and this baked potata'
This sublime and supreme
Unconventional team
This Mabel and Mack …

Also called Mack and Mabel

The perfect mix of oil and water
We're Svengali's son and Trilby's daughter
When she mugs and she wiggles
The world gets the giggles
But look in the wings
At who's pullin' the strings …

One fine morning we were introduced by fate
This goddam genius and this girl who counts
   to eight!

So, Sennett and his great creation
Are a damned unholy combination
Just a sweet little plum
And a big Irish bum
This Mabel and Mack

Also called Mack and Mabel!

▼ Bernadette Peters and Robert Preston.

WHEREVER HE AIN'T

This ninny of a puppet was available the
   second that he called!
And all he had to do was yell "Hey, Mabel" and
   this dumb hash-slinger crawled!
For seven lousy years I've watched him swear
   and shove and shout
"With you or without you!"
Well it's gonna be without

I gotta give my life some sparkle and fizz
And think a thought that isn't wrapped up
   in his
The place that I consider paradise is
Wherever he ain't! Wherever he ain't!

No more to wither when he's grouchy and gruff
No more to listen to him bellow and bluff
Tomorrow morning I'll be struttin' my stuff
Wherever he ain't! Wherever he ain't!

Enough of being bullied and bossed
Ta-ta, auf Wiedersehen, and get lost!

I walked behind him like a meek little lamb
And had my fill of his not givin' a damn
I'll go to Sydney or Ceylon or Siam
Wherever he ain't! Wherever he ain't!

It's time for little Nell to rebel
If he's in heaven, I'll go to hell!

I'd gladly travel where the hurricanes blow
I'd face the jungle and I'd stomp through
   the snow
As long as I can pack my baggage and go
Wherever he ain't
Wherever he ain't

My little love nest was a terrible trap
With me behaving like a simpering sap
And so I'm looking for a spot on the map
If he's goin' south
I'm goin' north
If he's goin' back
I'm goin' forth
Wherever he ain't!

James Mitchell and Bernadette Peters.

MACK AND MABEL This was added to the
original score years later for the London production. It gave the
audience a chance to see Mack and Mabel happy and playful together
before "the trouble begins." — J.H.

HUNDREDS OF GIRLS

I'll make a star and a half out of that one
The one with the dimples, the redhead, the
    fat one
How 'bout the one on the blanket, the one
    playing ball
Let's take 'em both … ah to hell with it
Let's take 'em all!

What gives a man
Ginger and snap
Goin' through life
With his little ol' lap
Full of hundreds and hundreds of girls

What gives a man
Power and punch
Tina for breakfast
And Lena for lunch
Having hundreds and hundreds of girls

Show him a blonde
And something in his soul will leap to respond
But then again he's also terribly fond
Of this brunette and so
Instead of one dandy dish
Pass him the candy dish

I'll sprinkle spice
Into his life
To make him forget
That he's stuck with his wife
Give him hundreds and hundreds of girls!

Beulah and Belle
Gladys and Gert
Two for the entree
And three for dessert
Give 'em hundreds and hundreds of girls

Four on a slide
Five on a swing
I'm gonna make
The cash register ring
Having hundreds and hundreds of girls

I'll fill the screen
With Jan and Jane and Joan and Janet and Jean
I'll pull the greatest stunt this business has
    seen
Till ev'ry fella from Duluth to Atlanta sees
All of his fantasies!

Analysts find
This thing called modern man was never
    designed
With only one eternal partner in mind
And so I gotta yell, "To hell with propriety
Viva variety"

Sinner or saint
Schoolgirl or queen
One girl is boring
And two are obscene
Give me hundreds and hundreds and hundreds
And hundreds of girls!

◀ "Hundreds of Girls" on the slide (Rita Rudner at bottom).

WHEN MABEL COMES IN THE ROOM

Somehow the ceiling
Seems a little higher
From the very moment I see Mabel come in
    the room
It feels like someone
Lit a roaring fire
But it's just the glow I get when Mabel comes
    in the room
The faded sofa
Stands a little prouder
That bunch of artificial flowers might even
    bloom
I can feel my heartbeat
Beat a little louder
The very moment I see Mabel come in the
    room

The dingy curtains
Seem a little brighter
I can hear the tinny piano playin' a gorgeous
    song
The grouchy doorman
Seems a bit politer
It's his way of saying, "Welcome home, you've
    been gone too long"
The day you left us
Was a small disaster
You took the love and light and laughter and
    left the gloom
But I can feel my heartbeat
Beat a little faster
And I can swiftly shed the strain of the years
The very moment her first footstep appears
The very moment I see Mabel come in the room

The threadbare carpet
Seems a little thicker
From the very moment I see Mabel come
    through the door
The elevator
Runs a little quicker
Just as if it didn't want to stop at another floor
The kids from Keystone
Are the kids no longer
We miss just having you around and the old
    rapport
But I can feel my heartbeat
Beat a little stronger
And I can swiftly shed the strain of the years
The very moment her first footstep appears
The very moment I see . . .

Mabel!

The faded sofa
Stands a little prouder
That bunch of artificial flowers might even
    bloom
I can feel my heartbeat
Beat a little louder
And I can swiftly shed the strain of the years
The very moment her first footstep appears
The very moment I see Mabel come in . . .
The room!

The cast sings "When Mabel Comes in the Room." ►

▲ Lisa Kirk, Tom Batten, Bernadette Peters, Robert Preston, Jerry Dodge (behind Preston's shoulder), Robert Fitch, and Nancy Evers.

▲ Bernadette Peters hangs by a pole in a scene cut out of town.

HIT 'EM ON THE HEAD It amused me to write a song celebrating the fact that Mack Sennett, without knowing it, introduced screen violence. — J.H.

HIT 'EM ON THE HEAD

Ev'ry time a cop falls down
My spirits soar
I'm in heaven when a flatfoot hits the floor
Billy clubs and nightsticks make me feel
Happy as a new born pup
'Cause ev'ry time a cop falls down
My heart leaps up!

Hit 'em on the head
Ha ha ha
Kick 'em in the shins
Ha ha ha
The heroine's behind
Is oh so ripe for bruising
Lash 'em in the loin
Ha ha ha
Grind 'em in the groin
Ha ha ha
Audiences find
That pain is so amusing
Everybody loves a little rabbit punching
Everybody loves the sound of knuckles
    crunching
So flatten someone's nose
Ha ha ha
Stub somebody's toes
Ha ha ha
Make a little thud
Draw a little blood
Hit 'em on the head!

Cause a little wreck
Ha ha ha
Break somebody's neck
Ha ha ha
Shoot a little gun
Yes, folks, it's scintillating
Watch the fella reel
And slip on that banana peel
The public finds it fun
When it's excruciating
Everybody loves to see policemen futile
In breaking up a brawl
That's been divinely brutal
So bite 'em in the calf
Ha ha ha
Listen to 'em laugh
Ha ha ha
Make a little slash
Make a little gash
Hit 'em on the head!
People just adore a fight that's death defying
Love it even more when there are bullets flying
So thrash 'em in the thigh
Ha ha ha
Blacken someone's eye
Ha ha ha
Get 'em in the gut
Bruise 'em on the butt
Make a little slash
Make a little gash
Bite 'em on the calf
Listen to 'em laugh
Hit 'em on the head!

TIME HEALS EVERYTHING

Time heals everything
Tuesday
Thursday
Time heals everything
April
August
If I'm patient the break will mend
And one fine morning the hurt will end
So make the moments fly
Autumn
Winter
I'll forget you by
Next year
Some year
Though it's hell that I'm going through
Some Tuesday
Thursday
April
August
Autumn
Winter
Next year
Some year
Time heals everything
Time heals everything
But loving you

Make the moments fly
Autumn
Winter
I'll forget you by
Next year
Some year
Though it's hell that I'm going through
Some Tuesday
Thursday
April
August
Autumn
Winter
Next year
Some year
Time heals everything
Time heals everything
But loving you

TIME HEALS EVERYTHING A carefully built
lyric of strength and determination that quietly explodes and becomes
heartbreaking with its last three words. I really love this song. — J.H.

Bernadette Peters and James Mitchell in the scene prior to
"Time Heals Everything." ▶

TAP YOUR TROUBLES AWAY

Tap your troubles away
You've bounced a big check
Your mom has the vapors
Tap your troubles away
Your car had a wreck
They're serving you papers
When you're the one that it always rains on
Simply try putting your Mary Janes on
The boss just gave you the ax
There's years of back tax
You simply can't pay
If a sky full of crap
Always lands in your lap
Make a curtsy and
Tap your troubles away

Tap your troubles away
You're sued for divorce
Your brother gets locked up
Tap your troubles away
You're fat as a horse
And find that you're knocked up
When you need something to turn your
    mind off
Why not try tapping your poor behind off?
Your boat goes over the falls
The plane you're on stalls
The pilot yells "Pray"
When your parachute strap
Is beginning to snap
Smile a big smile
And tap! Tap! Tap! Tap! Your troubles away

▲ Lisa Kirk encourages the audience to "Tap Your Troubles Away."

Tap your troubles away
A raging typhoon
An earthquake in Java
Tap your troubles away
The rats in Rangoon
The oncoming lava
Some people constantly take a licking
But you'll never know when your cleats are
    clicking
So through the mud and the mire
Through flood and through fire
Sincerely I say
When the wolf's at the door
There's a bluebird in store
If you glide cross the floor
Till your ankles get sore
Just tap your troubles away!
Your troubles away!
Your troubles away!

TAP YOUR TROUBLES AWAY took me back to my revue days. I used this spoof of 1920ish cheer-up songs as a background for the most serious scene in *Mack and Mabel.* — J.H.

I PROMISE YOU A HAPPY ENDING

I promise you a happy ending
Like the ones that you see on the screen
So if you've had a bad beginning
Love will come out winning
In the closing scene
And when you find it rough contending
With the grind that the world puts us through
I can promise you a happy ending
That has you ... loving me ... loving you

I promise you a happy ending
Like the one you've been dreaming about
Where vows are vowed
And knots are knotted
And the preacher's potted
As the reel runs out
And so I'm strongly recommending
That you pack up your old point of view
I can promise you a happy ending
That has you ... loving me ... loving you

▲ Robert Preston sings "I Promise You a Happy Ending."

I WON'T SEND ROSES - FINALE

In me you'll find things
Like guts and nerve
But not the kind things
That you deserve
But as the years go tumbling by
You never know
I might send roses ...

▼ Robert Preston, Jerry Dodge, and Bernadette Peters in "I Won't Send Roses—Finale."

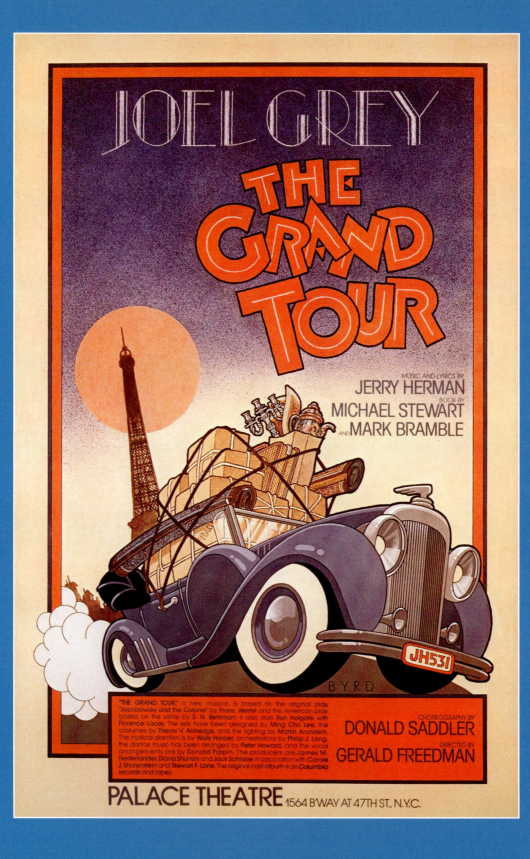

7

THE GRAND TOUR

Jerry Herman was convinced by frequent collaborator Michael Stewart, along with coauthor Mark Bramble, into undertaking this musical retelling of the 1944 comedy *Jacobowsky and the Colonel* by Franz Werfel. When the show underwent the usual birth pangs out-of-town, the lack of a strong, guiding hand at the top tipped the balance of power from the producer and director to the show's star, Joel Grey. By the time it had reached New York, *The Grand Tour* became more of a star vehicle than a well-integrated musical.

The show opened at Broadway's Palace Theatre on January 11, 1979. In a further departure from his *Dolly!* and *Mame* style, Jerry Herman wrote an understated, emotional score that still gleamed with his trademarked optimistic outlook.

Audiences and critics had, by this time, stereotyped him as a jaunty, razzle-dazzle writer of brash showstoppers. A victim of his own success with *Dolly!* and *Mame*, they forgot the many deeply touching moments he had also bestowed on all his shows. What they forgot is that for all the bright lights and belting choruses, his shows would never had achieved success if there had not been true heartfelt emotions at their centers.

Despite the mixed reviews of critical drubbing and real raves *The Grand Tour* was nominated for three Tony Awards, for Best Actor – Joel Grey, Best Supporting Actor – Ron Holgate and for Best Score.

The Grand Tour remains the least known of Jerry Herman's scores, overshadowed by the failings of its original production. It's another Herman score, which T.E. Kalem in *Time Magazine* called "as romantic as candlelight and wine," that deserves to be rediscovered through a new, well-focused production. — K.B.

▲▲▲▲▲▲▲▲▲▲▲▲▲▲▲▲▲▲▲▲▲▲▲▲▲▲▲▲▲▲▲▲▲▲▲▲▲▲▲

Jerry and Joel. ▶

I'LL BE HERE TOMORROW

Mama took the dishes
The furniture
Mama took the pillows
The candlesticks
Mama took the children
And fled to Berlin ...
I grew into manhood
A citizen
I went into business
A patriot
Foolishly believing
I belonged in Berlin ...

(spoken) *My incurable optimism!*

That knock on the door
In the dead of the night
And that voice saying
Run, the sky is falling
Run, the ship is sinking
Through the blind confusion
I remember still what I was
    thinking ...

I'll be here tomorrow
Alive and well and thriving
I'll be here tomorrow
My talent is surviving
If before the dawn this fragile
    world might crack
Someone's gotta try to put the
    pieces back
So, from beneath the rubble
You'll hear a little voice
Say "Life is worth the trouble"
Have you a better choice?
So let the skeptics say
"Tonight we're dead and gone"

I'll be here tomorrow
Simply going on!

We moved to Vienna
The city of waltzes
Of strudels and glitter and
    gold
We moved to Vienna
But under the waltzes
A strange countermelody
Ruthless and cold—
Run, your life's in danger
Run, you've been defeated
Racing through the night
I looked up at the stars as I
    repeated ...

I'll be here tomorrow
Alive and well and thriving
I'll be here tomorrow
My talent is surviving
If before the dawn this fragile
    world might crack
Someone's gotta try to put the
    pieces back
So, from beneath the rubble
You'll hear a little voice
Say "Life is worth the trouble"
Have you a better choice?
So let the skeptics say
"Tonight we're dead and gone"
I'll be here tomorrow
Simply going on!

To Paris
To Paris
The city of freedom and
    wonder and music and light
But even
In Paris
I'm dreading that knock on
    the door
In the dead of the night—
Run, the sky is falling
Run, the ship is sinking
When that moment happens
You know very well what I'll
be thinking ...

(music)

Someone's gotta try to put the
    pieces back
So, from beneath the rubble
You'll hear a little voice
Say "Life is worth the trouble"
Have you a better choice
So let the skeptics say
"Tonight we're dead and gone"
I'll be here tomorrow
Simply going on!

I'LL BE HERE TOMORROW After 9/11, I realized I had written
a song in 1979 that is much more pertinent today. This song has become my credo. — J.H.

TWO POSSIBILITIES

Two possibilities
Two possibilities
Life always offers you two
    possibilities
One way is sunny and the
    other way is shady
If the left is the tiger, than the
    right might be the lady
So, life has more spice in it
Life has more salt in it
When each prerogative offers
    an alternate
There's an escape hatch you
    can always use
With two possibilities … two
All you're required to do
Is choose.

You meet an exquisite young
    girl whose fancy you take
In the moonlight
You have too much wine and you
    make a horrendous mistake
In the moonlight
(spoken) Two possibilities.
She could become pregnant
Then again she could not
    become pregnant
It's bad if she's pregnant, that's
    true
But life is still offering you
The convenience of two
    possibilities
It could look exactly like her
Then again it could not look
    exactly like her
A boy with my face could be
    worse

But a girl with my face is a
    curse
But even a girl with a curse
Has the blessing of two
    possibilities
*(spoken) She could play the piano
beautifully.*

One way is enmity
One way is amity
One way is bound to be less
    the calamity
When you're presented with a
    lighted fuse
With two possibilities … two
All you're required to do
Is choose.

Two possibilities
Two possibilities
Life always offers you two
    possibilities
One way is sunny and the
    other way is shady
If the left is the tiger, then the
    right might be the lady
So, life has more spice in it
Life has more salt in it
When each prerogative offers
    an alternate
There's an escape hatch you
    can always use
With two possibilities … two
All you're required to do
Is choose.

The Germans might invade
    Paris
Then again, they might not
    invade Paris
If they do invade Paris we run
But I'll bet you a million to one
That even those sons of the Hun
Will bestow us with two
    possibilities
We could go to a good detention
    camp
Or to a bad detention camp
The camp may be urban or
    rural
But at least the perspective is
    plural
And what we might have to
    endure'll
Be tempered by two possibilities

Remember
Life has more spice in it
Life has more salt in it
When each prerogative offers
    an alternate
There's an escape hatch you
    can always use
With two possibilities … two
All you're required to do
Is choose!

TWO POSSIBILITIES A good example of losing the heart of a character by recklessly cutting a song on the road that told more about this man than pages and pages of dialogue. This lyric <u>is</u> S.L. Jacobowsky — J.H.

FOR POLAND

My code of honor says "Men are brothers"
That I should spread my arms and hug the
    world en masse
Love God almighty above all others
Who had the wisdom to have made me upper
    class
That I'm a man who loves his neighbors is an
    undisputed fact
But you, my friend, make prejudice an
    honorable act!
As I'm who I am, you are who you are
So I will not sit beside you in this car!

    At least, do it for Poland
    For a meal of pirogi and bigos
    And babka and tea
    And this pleasant little ride
    Can bring you patriotic pride
    If you do it for P-O-L-A-N-D
    Come on, do it for Poland
    For keeping the fatherland out and the
        motherland free
    Though your attitude is stoic
    They'll consider you heroic
    If you do it for P-O-L-A-N-D

I also honor the female gender
And show them my respect in every deed
    and thought
And my male ethics, in all their splendor
Say "Only be unfaithful if you don't get caught"
I may have stooped to indiscretion to secure a
    lady's kiss
But I never thought that I would have to stoop
    as low as this . . .

    At least, do it for Poland
    So the sausage'll keep getting stuffed and
        the sheep'll get shorn
    And you'll soon exchange your pallor
    For the rosy glow of valor
    When you do it for the land where you were born
    Come on, do it for Poland
    Paderewski, Pilsudski, and Chopin would
        surely agree
    That this deed that you are doubting
    Will become a summer outing
    When you do it for P-O-L-A-N-D
    For the folks in Gdynia
    It's a peach of a town
    For the men in the salt mines
    We can't let them down!

All right I'll do it for Poland
For keeping the fatherland out and the
    motherland free
The horrendous trip I'm taking
And the sacrifice I'm making
I'll be making for P-O-L-A-N-D

    For General Pulaski!
    For Kosciusko!
    For Vilna Gubernia!
    I'll be making for P-O-L-A-N-D

I BELONG HERE

I belong here
Where a dusty road curls by
Yes, I belong here
Where the birches touch the sky
There's nothing splendid
Or remarkable in any way
But I open the shutter each day
And it dazzles my eye …
There's a schoolhouse
And a noisy country store
A hill of lilac
And a bridge and not much more
And so if one day
To the ends of the earth I may roam—
I'll still belong here
I'll belong here;
On this speck of earth I call home!

▲ Florence Lacey sings "I Belong Here" to Chevi Colton.

I BELONG HERE My beautiful friend Florence
Lacey at her peak with this song. — J.H.

◀ Joel Grey takes a barge down the Seine.

MARIANNE

Don't ever tell me that you've heard the cello
For you've never met Marianne
Don't talk of silver or violet or yellow
For you've never met Marianne
Don't mention garnets or pearls from Manila
Forget them as fast as you can
Don't speak of ginger or lime or vanilla
Until you have kissed Marianne

Don't ever mention the lights from the planets
For you've never seen Marianne
You'll pity the Jennies, the Janes, and the
    Janets
The moment you've seen Marianne
And so the one thing I'm positive of is
That God made me one lucky man
Gentlemen, sorry ... you won't know what
    love is
Until you have loved Marianne!

MARIANNE I used romantic images ... sounds, colors, jewels, and scents to describe a girl. Certainly one of my most romantic lyrics. — J.H.

▼ Florence Lacey as Marianne.

I WANT TO LIVE EACH NIGHT

I want to live each night like it's my last one
Throw discretion to the wind
And when the foe is sighted and the sky's
    ignited
I'll be so delighted that I sinned this evening

If my life's to be a fast one, I implore you not
    to cry
Just hold me in your arms forevermore
And when you leave be sure to slam the door
And know you've helped a lady kiss the world
    good-bye!

I want to live each night like there's no morning
Just surround me with my men
And if I'm in a crisis, I'll recall my vices
And be glad my prices weren't any higher

When the gunshots sound their warning, and
    the rifles pierce the sky
Just tell me that you love me till you die
And promise me, darling, that you'll lie
And know you've helped a lady kiss the world
    good-bye!

If my life's to be a fast one, I implore you not
    to cry
And when this crazy town is laid to rest
I'll still be doing what I do the best
And when I say farewell I want it known
My very last position will be prone
And know you've helped a lady kiss the world
    good-bye!

I WANT TO LIVE EACH NIGHT was cut from *The Grand Tour* and reworked for the score of *Miss Spectacular.* However, it has just been cut from that show but "as God is my witness" you'll hear this one day. — J.H.

▼ *(following pages)* The cut brothel scene with (left to right): Debra Lyman, Bonnie Young, Jo Speros (kneeling), Travis Hudson, Florence Lacey, Tina Paul, Jay Stuart (on bar stool), Linda Poser, Mark Waldrop, and Michelle Marshall.

WE'RE ALMOST THERE

This old train
Is poor and tired
So your cooperation is urgently required
Although we're all embarking on a long and
   dismal trip
It's not too bad if you just add some French
   stiff upper lip

We're almost there
We're almost there
Though there's a million more kilometers to go
The window clatters
The engine spatters
But with a glass of wine, you'll never know
A spicy joke
A hand of bridge
And we'll forget the trip is tedious and slow
The car is musty
The track is rusty
We'll end up God knows where
But with diversion
It's an excursion!
And so we're almost there!

We're almost there
We're almost there
We're gonna wheel our way to St. Nazaire or bust
The air is choking
The gears are smoking
But in our engineer (and God) we trust
A little stroll
From car to car
And we'll forget about the danger and the dust
The roof is leaking
The wheels are shrieking
But we say c'est la guerre
There's Hell before
But one more chorus

And look—we're almost there!
We're almost there
We're almost there

We must arrive before the Roquefort gets
   too strong
Some conversation
Some recreation
Perhaps madame might offer us a song

A little bread
A little Brie
To help forget the trip's too languid and
   too long
The motor grumbles
A cannon rumbles
And gives us quite a scare
It's rough and risky
But have a whiskey
And look—we're almost there!

This old train
Is poor and tired
So your imagination is urgently required
See that quaint old factory in yonder glade
That's the place where Louis Fifteenth chairs
   are made

And on the left
That great big blur
I promise you that that's the back of the
   Sacre Coeur
That poplar played a noble role in history
Napoleon relieved himself behind that tree

That curl of smoke
That stains the sky
Would you believe that comes from a chimney
    at Versailles?
And see that lovely horse that's grazing there at
    the gate
The grandpa of that horse made love to
Catherine the Great
I tell you
This old train
Is quite a mess
But if you close your eyes you're on the Orient
    Express!

We're almost there
We're almost there
Though there's a million more kilometers to go
The window clatters
The engine spatters
But with a glass of wine, you'll never know
A spicy joke
A hand of bridge
And we'll forget the trip is tedious and slow
The car is musty
The track is rusty
We'll end up God knows where
But with diversion
It's an excursion!
And so we're almost there!

▼ Joel Grey assures (left to right) Carol Dorian, Steven Vinovich, Gene Varrone, Theresa Rakov, and Travis Hudson "We're Almost There."

MORE AND MORE/LESS AND LESS

Isn't he witty?
Doesn't he make you smile?
He's clever and resilient
Haven't you noticed
His continental style
His repartee is brilliant
His sense of honor
His sense of humor
His sense of order and plan
Poet and preacher,
Scholar and teacher
My little Renaissance man!
So much potential
He has to still explore
A genie in a bottle
If they would listen
He could resolve the war
My Polish Aristotle
His allure
His charm, and his candor
Make this tour
Seem grander and grander
Moment to moment
I like him more and more!

Less and less
I like this Jacobowsky
My contempt
The fellow is beneath
More and more
Those irritating ways of his
That sugarcoated glaze of his
Is rotting my back teeth
(He gives me indigestion)
When he smiles
He aggravates my sinus
When he laughs

He gives me nervous stress
She thinks he's cuddly as a pup
I think I'm going to throw up
More and more
I like him less and less

sung in counterpoint

Isn't he witty?	Less and less
Doesn't he make you smile?	I like this Jacobowsky
He's clever and resilient	My contempt
Haven't you noticed his	The fellow is beneath
continental style	
His repartee is brilliant	More and more
His sense of honor, his sense	Those irritating ways of his
of humor	
His sense of order and plan	That sugarcoated glaze of his
Poet and preacher, scholar and	Is rotting my back teeth
teacher	
My little Renaissance man!	(He gives me indigestion)
So much potential he has to	When he smiles
still explore	
A genie in a bottle	He aggravates my sinus
If they would listen he could	When he laughs
resolve the war	
My Polish Aristotle	He gives me nervous stress
His allure, his charm, and his	She thinks he's cuddly as a pup
candor	
Make this tour seem grander	I think I'm going to throw up
and grander	
Moment to moment	More and more
I like him more and more!	I like him less and less

▼Joel Grey and Florence Lacey sing "More and More/Less and Less."

ONE EXTRAORDINARY THING

Walk the highest wire
Do one extraordinary thing
Jump the ring of fire
Do one extraordinary thing
Make the crowd applaud the skill and the daring
Of the frightened fellow in the main ring
Though you may admire
The feats that other men have done
You top them all when you do one
Extraordinary thing

Make the mountain move
Do one extraordinary thing
Life's worth more when you've
Done one extraordinary thing
Reach the farthest spot out on the horizon
Make your wildest dreams wake up and
    take wing
You can always prove
You've earned your moment in the sun
When you can proudly point to one
Extraordinary thing!

When your strength is failing and you can't
    continue
Use that power you don't even know is in you

Catch the winning ball
Do one extraordinary thing
Scale the castle wall
Do one extraordinary thing
Slay the dragon for the hand of the princess
Bring the flag of vict'ry back to the king
Never envy all
The races other people run
The crown is yours for doing one
Extraordinary thing

Negative vibrations
From now on reject them
Miracles can happen
When you least expect them

Change tomorrow's course
Do one extraordinary thing
With inhuman force
Do one extraordinary thing
Sail the skies and plumb the depths of the
    ocean
Thrill the world and make the universe sing
Have no great remorse
For all the deeds you've never done
As long as you accomplish one …
Extraordinary thing!!

▼ Florence Lacey.

I THINK, I THINK

I think, I think I know the way it is
To be a Jacobowsky
I think I know the longing and the loneliness
That laugh of his conceals
I think the thoughts I think are just like his
This little Jacobowsky
I too know what it's like to be the prey
And have the hunter at my heels

I too have smiled at the danger
Pretending life doesn't hurt
I too have dreamed of the sunlight
And had to hide in the dirt

I think I used to think "How very sad
To be a Jacobowsky"
I think it's very far that I have traveled
Since this traveling began
Today I think I think it's not so bad
To be a Jacobowsky
I think I think someone so much like me
Must be a very special man!

I THINK, I THINK I thought it would be particularly telling to feel the Colonel's change of heart by his singing, "I think I think someone so much like me must be a very special man." — J.H.

Ron Holgate sings "I Think, I Think" to Florence Lacey. ▶

YOU I LIKE

You I like
So let me tip my hat
In your path
I spread my welcome mat
You I like
Can you imagine that?
Although your ways may be strange
And there's much that I'd change
Somehow
You I like
And warmly recommend
From now on
We'll call each other friend
I'll be at your side until the end
Can you believe that I've found
Such a thrill in the sound
Of the new chord we strike
You I like!

▼ Ron Holgate, Florence Lacey, Steven Vinovich, Joel Grey, and Lulu (the bird) sing the "You I Like."

◀ Ron Holgate and Joel Grey
discover that "You I Like."

I BELONG HERE - REPRISE

I belong here
Where my world is safe from harm
Yes, I belong here
On your reassuring arm
Though I may wander
To a far and remarkable place
With just one little look at your face
I'm at peace and at home
Let the whole world
Search for fortune and for fame
But I won't answer
When the west wind calls my name
And let the whole world
Travel on to a faraway star
But I belong here
I belong here
I belong wherever you are!

▲ Florence Lacey sings "I Belong Here" (Reprise) to Ron Holgate.

◀ Joel Grey and Lulu (the bird) with a reprise of "Marianne."

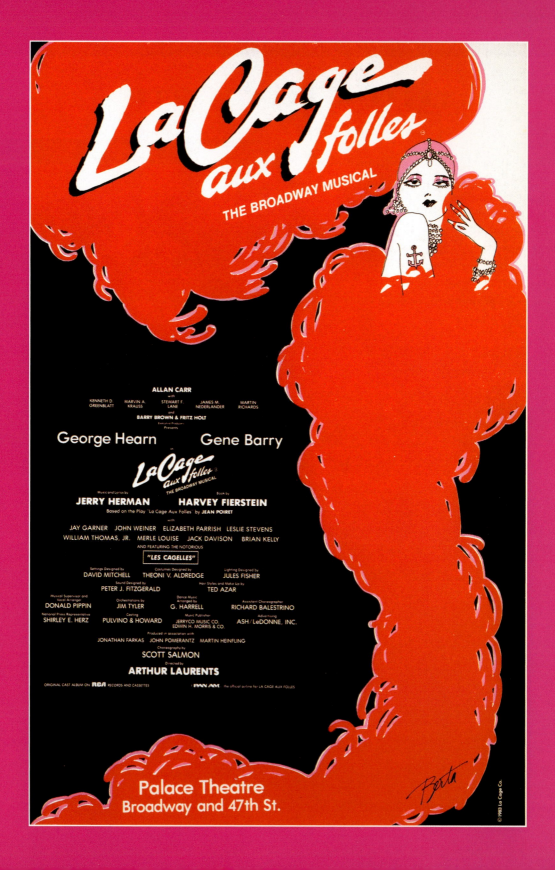

8

LA CAGE AUX FOLLES

Realizing what was expected of him by audiences and acknowledging the critical receptions of his more adventurous pieces, Jerry Herman came up with a plan to have his cake and eat it too. Along with librettist Harvey Fierstein, Jerry undertook the task of musicalizing the popular French play by Jean Poiret, *La Cage Aux Folles*. With equal doses of Broadway splash and political astuteness, *La Cage Aux Folles* achieved the miracle of succeeding on both fronts.

Although the farcical story ostensibly concerns itself with a clash of cultures, the book and score, together with director Arthur Laurents's sensitive direction, made what could have been seen as a polemic for gay rights into a universal story—a paean to individuality and the freedom of self-expression.

Jerry's score and Harvey's funny and touching libretto accomplished the difficult task of making the show's themes palatable to an audience

LA CAGE AUX FOLLES

who was just looking for a fun night at the theatre. By sweetening the message without apology he made more of an impact than he ever could have with mere rhetoric. "I Am What I Am" is written in the modern style of declarative anthems. But behind the bravado is a fully realized character who is driven to take a stand for himself—an idea to which all audiences could relate.

La Cage Aux Folles proved to audiences, critics, and Jerry Herman himself that, contrary to popular opinion, his style of Broadway heart and show biz was not out of date. *La Cage* swept the Tony Awards winning for Jerry Herman's score, Best Musical, Actor in a Musical—George Hearn (his costar, Gene Barry, was also nominated), Director, Best Book, and for Costumes—Theoni V. Aldredge. There were also nominations for Lighting—Jules Fisher and Choreography—Scott Salmon.

Following the smashing opening night performance of August 21, 1983, Jerry Herman walked out of the Palace Theatre onto Times Square. He knew he had nothing else to prove, he had shown his critics as well as his detractors that he could still write a big Broadway hit. And, with nothing else to prove, he vowed never to write another show for Broadway. — K.B.

▲▲▲▲▲▲▲▲▲▲▲▲▲▲▲▲▲▲▲▲▲▲▲▲▲▲▲▲▲▲▲▲

Gene Barry welcomes the audience to *La Cage Aux Folles.* ▶

WE ARE WHAT WE ARE

We are what we are
And what we are is an illusion
We love how it feels
Putting on heels
Causing confusion
We face life though it's sometimes sweet and
    sometimes bitter
Face life, with a little guts and lots of glitter
Look under our frocks: girdles and jocks
Proving we are what we are

We are what we are
Half a brassiere
Half a suspender
Half real and half fluff
You'll find it tough
Guessing our gender
So just (whistle)
If we please you that's the way to show us
Just (whistle)
'Cause you'll love us once you get to know us
Look under our glitz: muscles and tits
Proving we are what we are

WE ARE WHAT WE ARE I had a field day
with this material! It poured out of me as quickly and freely as a
runaway train. I wondered if I could get away with "look under our
glitz: muscles and tits" in 1983. Who knew what lay ahead? — J.H.

▼ George Hearn, Gene Barry, and the Cagelles.

A LITTLE MORE MASCARA I wanted
the audience to understand why Albin had the overwhelming need to
transform himself into Zaza. This song not only accomplishes that but
also provides the delicious spectacle of watching a middle-aged man in
a kimono become a dazzling star. Boy, was this fun to write. — J.H.

A LITTLE MORE MASCARA

Once again I'm a little depressed by the tired
old face that I see
Once again, it is time to be someone who's
anyone other than me
With a rare combination of girlish excitement
and manly restraint
I position my precious assortment of powders
and pencils and paint

So whenever I feel that my place in the world
is beginning to crash
I apply one great stroke of mascara to my rather
limp upper lash
And I can cope again
Good god, there's hope again

When life is a real bitch again
And my old sense of humor has up and gone
It's time for the big switch again
I put a little mascara on

When I count my crow's feet again
And tire of this perpetual marathon
I put down the john seat again
And put a little mascara on

And everything's sparkle dust, bugle beads,
ostrich plumes
When it's a beaded lash that you look through
'Cause when I feel glamorous, elegant,
beautiful
The world that I'm looking at's beautiful too

When my little road has a few bumps again
And I need something level to lean upon
I put on my sling pumps again
And wham! This ugly duckling is a swan!

So when my spirit starts to sag
I hustle out my highest drag
And put a little more mascara on

And everything's ankle straps, marabou,
Shalimar!
It's worth sucking in my gut and girdling my
rear
'Cause ev'rything's ravishing, sensual, fabulous!
When Albin is tucked away, and Zaza is here!

When everything slides down the old tubes
again
And when my self-esteem has begun to drift
I strap on my fake boobs again
And literally give myself a lift
So when it's cold and when it's bleak
I simply rouge the other cheek
For I can face another day
In slipper satin lingerie
To make depression disappear
I screw some rhinestones on my ear
And put my brooches and tiara
And a little more mascara on!

Harvey Evans as Zaza in the national tour at the beginning of "A Little More Mascara." ▶

WITH ANNE ON MY ARM

Girls have come and gone, Papa
Angelique and Antoinette
Who did I prefer, Leslie or Helene?
It was all a blur, and yet, Papa
When Anne comes walking down the street
    and I link my arm in hers
Girls have come and gone, girls may come
    and go
But something very odd occurs, Papa … 'cause

Life is in perfect order with Anne on my arm
It makes my shoulders broader with Anne on
    my arm
Even when things won't gel, and the pieces
    won't fit
I'm suddenly in, I'm suddenly on, I'm
    suddenly "it"
Who else can make me feel like I'm handsome
    and tall?
Who else can make me feel I'm on top of it all?
I found a combination that works like a charm
I'm simply a man who walks on the stars
Whenever it's Anne on my arm

Life is a celebration with you on my arm
Walking's a new sensation with you on my arm
Each time I face a morning that's boring and
    bland
With you it looks great, with you it looks good,
    with you it looks grand!
Somehow, you've put a permanent star in my eye
Even the dead of winter can feel like July
We start a conflagration that's cause for alarm
We're giving off sparks, we're setting off bells
Whenever it's you on my arm
Who else can make me feel like I'm handsome
    and tall?
Who else can make me feel I'm on top of it all?
I found a combination that works like a charm
I'm simply a man who walks on the stars
Whenever it's Anne on my arm

◀ *(left page)* George Hearn's first appearance as Zaza at the end of
"Mascara." *(left)* Gene Barry watches while Leslie Stevens dances
and John Weiner sings "With Anne on My Arm."

WITH YOU ON MY ARM

Life is a celebration with you on my arm
It's worth the aggravation with you on my arm
Each time I face a morning that's boring and
   bland
With you it looks good, with you it looks great,
   with you it looks grand
Somehow you've put a permanent star in my eye
Even the dead of winter can feel like July
I found a combination that works like a charm
It's suddenly (kiss), it's suddenly aah!
Whenever it's you on my arm

▼ Gene Barry and George Hearn sing "With You on My Arm."

SONG ON THE SAND

Do you recall that windy little beach we
    walked along?
That afternoon in fall, that afternoon we met?
A fella with a concertina sang, what was the
    song?
It's strange what we recall, and odd what
    we forget

I heard la da da da da da da as we walked on
    the sand
I heard la da da da I believe it was early
    September
Through the crash of the waves I could tell that
    the words were romantic
Something about sharing
Something about always

Though the years race along I still think of our
    song on the sand
And I still try and search for the words I can
    barely remember
Though the time tumbles by there is one thing
    that I am forever certain of
I hear la da da da da da da da da da da da da
And I'm young and in love

I believe it was early September
Through the crash of the wave I could tell that
    the words were romantic
Something about sharing
Something about always

Though the years race along I still think of our
    song on the sand
And I still try and search for the words I can
    barely remember
Though the time tumbles by, there is one thing
    that I am forever certain of
I hear la da da da da da da da da da da da da da
And I'm young and in love

▼ *(top)* Gene Barry and George Hearn sing "Song on the Sand."
(bottom) Larry Kert and Harvey Evans sing "Song on the Sand."

SONG ON THE SAND When I came up with the
idea of two people in love trying to remember a song they had heard
at the beginning of their relationship and only recalling patches of the
lyric, this song became a joy to write. I had often walked along a beach
with someone I loved. Is there anything more romantic? — J.H.

LA CAGE AUX FOLLES

It's rather gaudy but it's also rather grand
And while the waiter pads your check he'll kiss
    your hand
The clever gigolos romance the wealthy
    matrons
At La Cage Aux Folles

It's slightly forties, and a little bit "New Wave"
You may be dancing with a girl who needs a
    shave
Where both the riff-raff and the royalty are
    patrons
At La Cage Aux Folles

La Cage Aux Folles, the maître d' is dashing
Cage Aux Folles, the hat check girl is flashing
We import the drinks that you buy
So the Perrier is Canada Dry

Eccentric couples always punctuate the scene
A pair of eunuchs and a nun with a marine
To feel alive you get a limousine to drive you
To La Cage Aux Folles

It's bad and beautiful, it's bawdy and bizarre
I know a duchess who got pregnant at the bar
Just who is who and what is what is quite a
    question
At La Cage Aux Folles

Go for the mystery, the magic and the mood
Avoid the hustlers, and the men's room and the
    food
For you get glamour and romance and indigestion
At La Cage Aux Folles

La Cage Aux Folles, a Saint-Tropez tradition
Cage Aux Folles, you'll lose each inhibition
All week long we're wondering who
Left a green Givenchy gown in the loo

You'll be so dazzled by the ambience you're in
You'll never notice that there's water in the gin
Come for a drink and you may wanna spend
    the winter at La Cage Aux Folles

Gene Barry. ▶

La Cage Aux Folles, a Saint-Tropez tradition
Cage Aux Folles, you'll lose each inhibition
We indulge each change in your mood
Come and sip your Dubonnet in the nude

You go alone to have the evening of your life
You meet your mistress, and your boyfriend,
    and your wife
It's a bonanza, it's a mad extravaganza
At La Cage Aux Folles

You cross the threshold and your bridges have
    been burned
The bar is cheering for the Duchess has
    returned
The mood's contagious; you can bring your
    whole outrageous entourage
It's hot and hectic, effervescent and eclectic
At La Cage Aux Folles!

▲ Zaza swings above the Cagelles in "La Cage Aux Folles."

The brilliant Kenn Duncan shot these photos for a proposed calendar of La Cage Aux Folles. Unfortunately, the calendar wasn't produced. This is the first time these wonderfully witty photos have been seen since they were taken in 1983.

The Cagelles:

David Cahn

Frank DiPasquale

John Dolf

David Engel

David Evans

Linda Haberman

Eric Lamp

Dan O'Grady

Deborah Phelan

Sam Singhaus

I AM WHAT I AM

I am what I am
I am my own special creation
So come take a look, give me the hook
Or the ovation
It's my world that I want to take a little pride in
My world, and it's not a place I have to hide in
Life's not worth a damn
'Til you can say "Hey world, I am what I am"

I am what I am
I don't want praise, I don't want pity
I bang my own drum, some think it's noise
I think it's pretty
And so what, if I love each feather and each
    spangle
Why not try to see things from a diff'rent
    angle?
Your life is a sham
'Til you can shout, out loud, "I am what I am"

I am what I am
And what I am needs no excuses
I deal my own deck, sometimes the ace
Sometimes the deuces
There's one life and there's no return and
    no deposit
One life, so it's time to open up your closet
Life's not worth a damn
'Til you can say, "Hey world, I am what I am!"

▲ Walter Charles sings "I Am What I Am."

I AM WHAT I AM I know it's become an anthem. I know it's become a pop disco favorite. But to me, it will always be a cry for help, brilliantly delineated by George Hearn, alone on stage, creating even more of a powerful theatrical experience than either *Dolly* or *Mame's* title songs. — J.H.

MASCULINITY

Think of this as
Masculine toast
And masculine butter
Think of this as ready for spreading by a
    masculine hand
Pick up the knife and make believe it's a
    machete
It'll take all your strength and steady nerves
For hacking your way through the cherry
    preserves

Think of John Wayne and John Paul Belmondo
Think of the Legionnaires and Charlemagne's
    men
So like a stevedore you grab your cup
And if God forbid that your pinky pops up
You can climb back up the mountain once again

Grunt like an ape and growl like a tiger
Give us a roaring, snorting masculine laugh
Try and remember that John Wayne was not
    soprano
Try keeping it rough and gruff and low

Ha, ha!

Try more of John Wayne and less Brigitte
    Bardot!

Think of de Gaulle and think of Rasputin
Think like a Daniel marching into the den
While trying to join the burly brutes
If you forget that your nylons are under your
    boots
You can climb back up the mountain once again

Think Ghengis Khan and think Taras Bulba
Think of Attila's Huns and Robin Hood's men
Try not to weaken or collapse
If they discover the petticoat under your chaps
You can climb back up the mountain once again

◀ Van Johnson and George Hearn
    sing "Masculinity."

Gene Barry and George Hearn. ▶

▼ George Hearn.

▼ The Cagelles in "La Cage Aux Folles."

LOOK OVER THERE

How often is someone concerned with the
    tiniest thread of your life?
Concerned with whatever you feel and
    whatever you touch?
Look over there, look over there
Somebody cares that much

How often does somebody sense that you need
    them without being told?
When you have a hurt in your heart you're too
    proud to disclose?
Look over there, look over there
Somebody always knows

When your world spins too fast
And your bubble has burst
Someone puts himself last
So that you can come first

So count all the loves who will love you from
    now 'til the end of your life
And when you have added the loves who have
    loved you before
Look over there, look over there
Somebody loves you more

When your world spins too fast
And your bubble has burst
Someone puts himself last
So that you can come first

So count all the loves who will love you from
    now 'til the end of your life
And when you have added the loves who have
    loved you before
Look over there, look over there
Somebody loves you more

▲ William Thomas Jr., Van Johnson, and John Weiner.

LOOK OVER THERE A songwriter only has a few chances in
a career to write a perfect lyric. This is my best shot. — J.H.

DISHES

— sung in four-part counterpoint —

[1]
I joined the Foreign Legion with a saber in
    my hand
I crawled across the desert with my belly in
    the sand
With men who loved their camels and their
    brandy and I swear
Nobody dished, nobody swished when I was a
Foreign Legionnaire

[2]
Oh, what lovely dishes! They're so delicate
    and frail
Mine have naked children; I believe they're
    only male
Oops! I think they're playing some exotic
    little game
Oops! I think that "Leapfrog" is its name

[3]
This is even worse than I feared
The son is strange
The father is weird
To meet the wife, I'm actually afraid
I prefer that Anne remain an old maid

[4]
It's appalling to confess
Our new in-laws are a mess
She's a prude, he's a prig
She's a pill, he's a pig
Zis zis zis for you Papa

The *La Cage Aux Folles* company on the steps of the Palace Theatre lobby. ▶

THE BEST OF TIMES

This is a little song enchanting and unique-eh!
I learned to sing this song before I learned to speak-eh!
I learned to sing this song upon my mother's knee
And she learned to sing this song upon her mother's knee
And her mother learned this song upon her mother's knee
And if your mother sang this song to you, then sing along with me ...

The best of times is now
What's left of summer but a faded rose?
The best of times is now
As for tomorrow, well, who knows, who knows, who knows?

So hold this moment fast
And live and love as hard as you know how
And make this moment last
Because the best of times is now, is now, is now

Now! Not some forgotten yesterday
Now! Tomorrow is too far away

So hold this moment fast
And live and love as hard as you know how
And make this moment last
Because the best of times is now, is now, is now
Is now!
Is now!

George Hearn and Elizabeth Parrish sing "The Best of Times." ▶

▲ The entire cast records "The Best of Times."

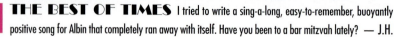

THE BEST OF TIMES I tried to write a sing-a-long, easy-to-remember, buoyantly positive song for Albin that completely ran away with itself. Have you been to a bar mitzvah lately? — J.H.

9

MRS. SANTA CLAUS

Jerry was reunited with Angela Lansbury for the original television musical, *Mrs. Santa Claus*. The 90-minute musical special premiered December 8, 1996, on CBS. The story of Mrs. Claus leaving the North Pole to discover the world at large and, in doing so, finds a new self-respect for her own identity might have been the usual holiday bonbon. But Jerry Herman and book writer Mark Saltzman slip in subtle messages about women's equality and the need for different cultures to coexist peacefully.

The score is light and deft, fitting with the show's holiday nature. If plans to mount the show on stage in London in 2004 as a Christmas pantomime come to fruition, Jerry Herman plans to write additional songs. — K.B.

MRS. SANTA CLAUS

I need something challenging to do
Somewhere marvelous to go
He's seen ev'ry little corner of the world
All I've ever seen is snow …

I'm Missus Santa Claus, the invisible wife
And Missus Santa Claus needs a change in
    her life
I've been manning the bus'ness and planning
    each holiday plan
And I'm tired of being the shadow behind the
    great man

For each December when Santa's checking
    his list
'Tis the season that he forgets I exist
So the moment has come to beat my own
    drum because
I want the world to know there's a Missus
    Santa Claus

I'm Missus Santa Claus, yes, I'm married
    to him
And for centuries I've been proper and prim
But I'm tired of folding the bedding and
    spreading the jam
And I feel I'm about to begin to find out
    who I am!

I've planned my strategy and my flag is
    unfurled
For I have gifts of my own to offer the world
So I'm coming your way, keep an eye on my
    sleigh because
I want the world to know there's a Missus
    Santa Claus!

So I'm coming your way
Keep an eye on my sleigh because
You'll have a merrier Christmas with
    Missus Santa Claus!

ALMOST YOUNG

I'm holding back the hands of time
And though a fool may say
I've passed my prime
My heart has always clung
To staying almost young

A few gray hairs, a few gold teeth
Can never hide the kid that's underneath
A kid whose hopes are hung
On staying almost young

My walk is swift and sporty
My disposition is evergreen
Why say, "I'm over forty"?
I'm over seventeen!

I'll still have all the speed it takes
When all the others have applied the brakes
And when my knell has rung
I'll still be struttin' and kickin' like some
    little chicken
And almost young

So if you think this spunky pup is either
    boggin' down or slowin' up
You'd better hold your tongue
I'm feeling almost young

My bones are often racked up, they always act
    up each time it rains
But my arthritis and my phlebitis are simply
    growing pains!
So let them say I've passed my peak
That I'm a million years from hide-and-seek
But when my dirge is sung
I'll still be tough as a riddle and fit as a fiddle
And struttin' and kickin' like some little chicken
And almost young!

▲ Angela Lansbury.

AVENUE A

Welcome to the world of Avenue A
Where you hear, "Come sta" and "Bless my
  soul" and "Oy vey!"
Rosie Finklestein and Michael Monihan are
  still going steady
Missus Brandenheim is yelling out the window,
  "Dinner is ready"

And that's the way it goes on Avenue A
Where Father Callahan bids Rabbi Hirsch
  a good day
Pickled herring and lasagna and chow mein
  all share the same tray
Part of the great big bouillabaisse called
  Avenue A

Welcome to the world of Avenue A
Where there's a new adventure waiting day
  after day
There's a secondhand emporium on ev'ry
  corner that I'd walk
Ring-a-levio and little girls with jacks all share
  the same sidewalk

And that's the way it goes on Avenue A
Look! There's a pushcart full of bagels coming
  your way
There's a ragman with a saxophone
There's not a tune he can't play
Part of the great kaleidoscope called Avenue A

I've landed in the world of Avenue A
Where you hear, "Come sta" and "Bless my
  soul" and "Oy vey!"
There's a ragman with a saxophone
There's not a tune he can't play
Part of the great kaleidoscope called Avenue A

AVENUE A It's not often that you get a chance to use
"oy vey" in a lyric. — J.H.

Angela Lansbury.

DEAR MRS. SANTA CLAUS

Dear Missus Santa Claus: wherever you are
I'm without you as lost as some little star
You're not there when I call and so ev'rything's
    all askew
So I guess, little wife, that the joy in my life
    is you

Dear Missus Santa Claus: how I hope you
    can see
From now on what a drastic change there
    will be
So I wish on the moon you come home to
    me soon because
You'll never know how Santa misses
    Missus Claus

▼ Angela Lansbury.

▲ *(previous pages)* Angela Lansbury.

WE DON'T GO TOGETHER AT ALL

A girl with a drive and a fellow with a dream
Are like pickled herring with vanilla ice cream
So as unromantic as my words may seem
We don't go together at all

My big loud mouth and your quiet ways
Are like August evenings with December days
Are like corned beef and cabbage topped
    with mayonnaise
We don't go together at all

We're like chicken soup and a slice of ham
We're the big bad wolf and the little lamb
Like a picnic lunch that's ruined by a
    sudden squall
We don't, no we don't, no we don't go
    together at all

Like a overcoat and a hot July
Like a bowl of borscht and a pizza pie
Like if I asked you to come to the policeman's
    ball
We don't, no we don't, no we don't go together
    at all

An onion roll at a Mayfair tea
Like a march by Sousa in a minor key
So forget all the magic that was meant to be
We don't go together at all

A stable boy and a suffragette
Are about as peculiar as a pair can get
So it's, oh, such a pity that we even met
We don't go together at all

But, I like your spunk and I like your pride
So I'll still be there marching at your side
So, I guess, my friend, we must admit the
    simple fact
That opposites, oh yes, opposites attract!

WHISTLE

Whistle
When you feel that no one is near
Whistle and you'll find me standing right here
Here to help smooth out the wrinkles, here to
    make loneliness end
It'll do you a lot of good, knowing you've got a
    good friend!

(And all you have to do is)
Whistle
And you'll find me holding your hand
When life doesn't go the way that you planned
Whatever rut you get stuck in, you'll feel me
    pulling you through
And then forevermore, you'll hear me whistling
    for you!

Whatever rut you get stuck in, you'll feel me
    pulling you through
And then and forevermore you'll hear me
    whistling for you!

HE NEEDS ME

Ev'ry little star that's falling
Means someone you love is calling . . .

He needs me
Yes, he needs me
Don't even ask me how I know
I know when he calls me
My heart hears him
And tells me that it's time for me to go

He's my world, and I am his
He's my world, and journey's end is where
    he is
And his laughter is my laughter
And tells me what I'm living for
And so, if he needs me, I'll go
'Cause I need him much more

He's my world, and I am his
He's my world, and journey's end is where
    he is
And his laughter is my laughter
And tells me what I'm living for
And so, if he needs me, I'll go
'Cause I need him much more

Angela Lansbury and Charles Durning. ▶

10

MISS SPECTACULAR

Jerry Herman's latest theatre project won't be opening on Broadway. Instead it will premiere in Las Vegas in 2004. Tommy Tune is set to direct. The show is about a young girl who dreams of becoming a Las Vegas showgirl. The score contains four lavish dream sequences in which she visualizes herself as Miss Spectacular. Jerry's contribution provides the glitter of *La Cage Aux Folles* with the heart of *Mame* and *Mack and Mabel.* — K.B.

MISS WHAT'S HER NAME

Miss What's Her Name, Miss Wanna Be
Has dozens of daydreams and hundreds of stars
    in her eyes
What's Her Name, just wait and see
Is due for that write-up predicting she'll light
    up the skies

So when one day the house lights dim
The curtains are parting, excitement is starting
    to grow
When you hear that applause
You'll know it's because
Miss What's Her Name is stopping the show!

Miss What's Her Name, Miss Needs a Break
In love with the clamor of opulent glamorous
    nights
My time has come, for goodness sake
My reason for being is seeing my name up in
    lights

So one great dream I dream each night
The audience roaring, the people adoring me so
When they holler, "Encore"
You'll know who it's for
Miss What's Her Name is stopping the show!

So one great dream I dream each night
The audience roaring, the people adoring me so
When they holler, "Encore"
You'll know who it's for
Miss What's Her Name is thrilling them
What's Her Name is killing them
What's Her Name is stopping the show!

LAS VEGAS

Vegas ... that great sensation
Where nothing is quite what it seems
Vegas ... a combination
Of thrills and excitement and dreams
Where ev'ry ordinary civilian
Can turn a half a buck into half a million
You'll find your cares are lighter
Whenever they turn on those lights
You won't know which is brighter
The stars or the star-studded nights
Come find a brand new girlfriend or bring
    your wife
Las Vegas will light up your life!

Come see an art collection
And buy a spectacular jewel
Dine on a rich confection
Then have a massage by the pool
There's nothing sad or sordid or seedy
You'll find romance and laughter and Steve
    and Eydie
Come hear a brilliant lecture
And dance to a cha-cha band
Gape at the architecture
It's "Fantasy Island" on land
Forget Atlantic City or Nice or Rome
You'll sit there forever
Just pulling that lever
Las Vegas ... you'll never go home!

LAS VEGAS The first song I wrote for the show. On the concept album Steve Lawrence himself sings the line about Steve and Eydie. — J.H.

ZIEGFELD GIRL

Ziegfeld Girl
Show us your crimson lips and sapphire eyes
Show us the beauty that your name implies
We'll never tire of watching you descend the stairs

Oh, Ziegfeld Girl
Show us the glamour that your name defined
Show us the figure that the gods designed
We'll never tire of watching you descend the stairs

We're hypnotized
By ev'ry graceful movement that you make
We're mesmerized
By ev'ry song you sing and ev'ry silken step you take

Oh, Ziegfeld Girl
We know you'll leave us in a little while
With just the mem'ry of your haunting smile
And just the thrill of watching you descend
Descend
Descend the stairs

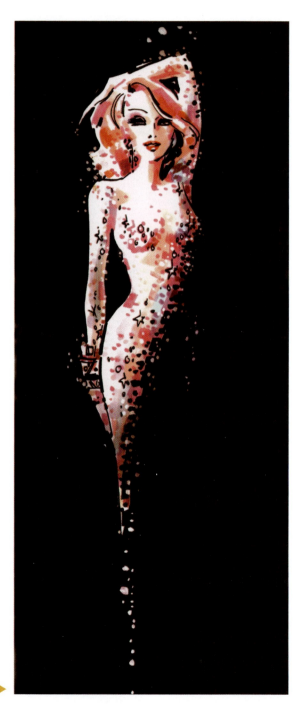

Costume design by Bob Mackie. ▶

SARAH JANE

I'll sing you an old-fashioned song
My Sarah Jane
A piano and violin song
An Irving Berlin song
Where the lyric calls you "Honey Lamb"
And if you go strollin' with me
Down lovers lane ...
You'll hear me say, I'll love you forever
My Sarah Jane

I'll sing you a rock-a-bye song
My Sarah Jane
A rousing Robert E. Lee song
A down on one knee song
Where you hear the banjos strummin'
And we'll leave for a honeymoon on
That Memphis train
So all aboard, I'll love you forever
My Sarah Jane

WHERE IN THE WORLD IS MY PRINCE?

I have countries and counties and physical
    bounties
And orchards and orchids and quince
I have barrels of rubies and breathtaking
    boobies
But where in the world is my prince?

Ev'ry day Neiman Marcus massages my carcass
Sassoon give my tresses a rinse
I've been trained by Nijinsky and coached
    by Lewinsky
So where in the world is my prince?

Then along came a man from a land that was
    far, far away
He was strong, he was smart, he was sweet, he
    was rich, he was gay!

I have ladies in waiting and *Forbes* highest
    rating
It shouldn't be hard to convince
Some young dude to devour me, to come and
    deflower me
Oh where in the world is my prince?

Then along came a man bearing gifts in a
    bucket of gold
He was strong, he was smart, he was sweet, he
    was rich, he was old!

And so while I've been sitting my stocks have
    been splitting
And gathering dust ever since
So, pray, come and corrupt me, seduce and
    abduct me
Come delve in my treasures, unspeakable
    pleasures
Oh where in the world is my prince?

So I learned watching Zsa Zsa please some
    maharaja
With tricks that could make a girl wince
Send a shy or a proud one, just one well-
    endowed one
Pray, someone starts calling before things start
    falling
Oh where in the world is my prince?

Send a shy or a proud one, just one well-
    endowed one
Pray, someone starts calling before things start
    falling
Oh where in the world is my prince?

WHERE IN THE WORLD IS MY PRINCE? I loved writing this song so much that I was almost saddened when it was finished! — J.H.

NO OTHER MUSIC

There's not a trace of Pavarotti in your throat
There's not a bit of Bing or Frank in any note
And yet the tune you hum each time you cross
    the floor
Gives me a feeling that I've never felt before, for

No other music takes my breath away
Only the magic of your song
Your la da da da da da da
Makes the voice in my heart sing along
And no other music has such majesty
No other mem'ry is as strong
Just sing that strain, that soft refrain
And the tunes in my ear
All at once disappear
And there's no other music but your sweet song

No other music has such majesty, no other
    mem'ry is as strong
Just sing that strain, that soft refrain
And the notes I have known
All have blurred, all have flown
And there's no other music but your sweet song

MISS SPECTACULAR

Look up, confetti's falling
And listen, the press is calling
It's more than I dreamed it would be
Miss Spectacular!
It's spectacular being me

And I see the banners waving
And I hear the people raving
And even the critics agree
Miss Spectacular!
It's spectacular being me

You won't believe the glorious feeling I feel
You'll say, "The girl is dreaming." But this
    time it's real!

I know that this time the trumpet's sounding
And this time my heart is pounding
And this time the whole world can see
Miss Spectacular!
It's spectacular being me

You won't believe the glorious feeling I feel
You'll say, "The girl is dreaming." But this
    time it's real!

I hear paparazzi flashing
They tell me that I look smashing
My Cartier necklace is free
Miss Spectacular!
It's spectacular being me

CD cover for *Miss Spectacular.* ▶

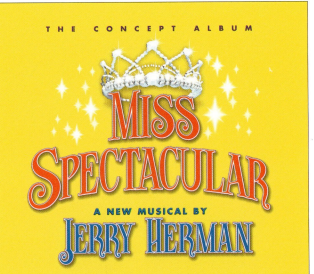

MY GREAT DREAM

My great dream is a simple dream
And the journey's not very far
Nothing grand or extravagant
Just a world that we can share, together
Just a quiet and simple life
Where we both can be what we are
Just a kid and a man and wife
In a house that's nestled by a stream
Just a little piece of sky
Just a room that's filled with love
And that's all there is to my
Great Dream

MY GREAT DREAM After all the glitz and the sequins that had been dancing in my head, it was lovely writing a lyric that was simple, straightforward, and grounded. — J.H.

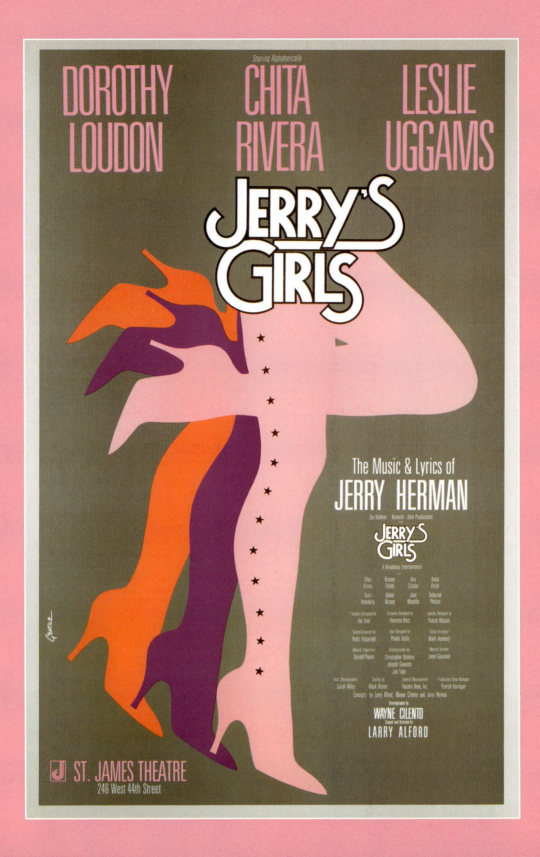

11

MISCELLANEOUS

Jerry also contributed individual songs to a few Broadway productions at the behest of their producers. Interpolations both with and without credit, have been a long tradition in the theatre. Writers such as Richard Rodgers, Stephen Sondheim, Frank Loesser, and Bock and Harnick supplied songs to Broadway shows without credit. Jerry was asked by Robert Preston to supply two songs for *Ben Franklin in Paris*.

When the Broadway producers of *A Day in Hollywood/A Night in the Ukraine* decided that the London transfer's score could use some beefing up, they asked Jerry Herman to supply the additional numbers.

Jerry's Girls was a revue made up of existing numbers from Jerry's shows. However, he was inspired to write one piece of special material, "Take It All Off," the lament of a stripper well past her prime.

Jerry also wrote two pieces of special material for benefits saluting Judy Garland and Mary Martin. He chose to set his lyrics to existing tunes. These songs remain funny and touching tributes to two of Jerry's favorite stars.   — K.B.

BEN FRANKLIN IN PARIS
TO BE ALONE WITH YOU

I'd sail the skies, off to the farthest little star,
    I'd go
Sail the skies and watch the people disappear
    below
I would gladly give up ev'ry earthly thing I
    know
To be alone with you
To be alone with you

I'd roam the earth and ev'ry corner of the
    Seven Seas
Roam the earth and search the spray of ev'ry
    salty breeze
I would let the raging oceans take me where
    they please
To be alone with you

To hold your hand in mine with nobody there
    beside us
To hold your hand in mine, there's nothing I
    wouldn't do

But if someday, to have to share you with the
    world I must,
If someday I find each plan of mine has turned
    to dust
Then while you're here, all that I want in all this
    world is just
To be alone with you

When I was asked to ghostwrite two songs for *Ben Franklin in Paris* for my pal Robert Preston, little did I know that I would meet the man who would become my musical director for the rest of my life, Don Pippin. Oliver Smith had designed a beautiful hot air balloon and basket that moved gently above the stage and I had to write something that made sense in that set. Hence, **TO BE ALONE WITH YOU**. And that's show business! — J.H.

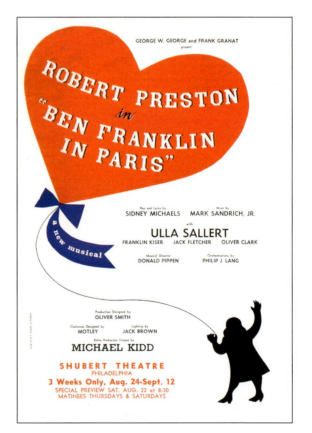

Robert Preston and Ulla Sallert sing "To Be Alone with You."

BEN FRANKLIN IN PARIS
TOO CHARMING

How do you do it
You still excite the same old hunger
So many years
But I swear Diane you're looking younger

You've always been too gallant to resist
Too gracious to conceive
You've always been too dashing to forget
And too charming to believe
You must remember your persuasive powers
I know
You're still exhilarating, scintillating,
    generating, palpitating
The answer is no

You've always been too ardent to restrain
Too noble to defeat
Our loving was too tender to reproach
And too charming to repeat
I know you well Ben; Lafayette and Moses
    combined
You're still rejuvenating, fascinating,
    captivating, devastating
And I won't change my mind

You've always been too gallant to resist
Too gracious to conceive
And too winning
Too gallant
Too noble
Too dashing
Too daring
Too charming to believe!

Robert Preston and Ulla Sallert. ▶

▼ Kate Draper, David Garrison, Peggy Hewett, Stephen James, Priscilla Lopez, and Frank Lazarus (at the piano) in *A Day In Hollywood*.

JUST GO TO THE MOVIES

Follow me down the aisle of the Grauman's
    Chinese Theatre
A colossal architectural sensation!
From the plush of your seat in the Grauman's
    Chinese Theatre
Life can be as plush as your imagination
So if pure entertainment's your style
Follow me, I have two on the aisle

Need to relax, need to escape
Go see Fay Wray in the palm of the ape
Watch Errol Flynn shooting his bow
Just go to the movies, just go to a picture show

Oh, when your morale needs some repairs
Watch Busby's beauties descending the stairs
Hundreds of girls doin' high kicks
Just go to the movies, just go to the flicks

And all for the sum of a quarter life is peachy
You can become Alice Faye or Don Ameche
Swamped with your bills? Late with your rent?
Watch Bette Davis run out on George Brent

See Fred Astaire steppin' in style
When ev'rything's dark and upset
Go calling on Clark and Claudette
Just go to a marvelous movie and smile!

Girls in sarongs, monsters in capes
See Scarlet make a dress out of the drapes
Life can be grand from the third row
Just go to the movies, just go to a picture show

Oh, Cooper in *Wings*, Crawford in *Rain*
See Tarzan beat his chest when he meets Jane
Sing with Dick Powell, ride with Tom Mix
Just go to the movies, just go to the flicks

Vicariously, you are flying down to Rio
Share the marquee with Missus Marx's zany trio

So, when your life seems a bit lean
Just let some shadows appear on the screen
Shine like a star for a brief while
Whenever you're down in the dumps
Try putting on Judy's red pumps

And visit Lugosi and Boris
The girls in the chorus
A dangerous beauty
A kewpie doll cutie
An ancient High Lama
A high-steppin' mama
Just go to the movies and smile!

JUST GO TO THE MOVIES Tommy Tune
was in Baltimore with *A Day in Hollywood* and called to ask for an
opening number about "the movies." It was after I said, "Sure, sounds
like fun" that he mentioned that he needed it in 24 hours. I used every
old Hollywood image I could think of and delivered it on time. — J.H.

A DAY IN HOLLYWOOD
NELSON

My heart, my love
My life is his alone
But if
But if
But if the truth be known

My hero must stand
On a box in our love scenes
And god does he act
Like a lox in our love scenes
Oh, Nelson
What you're putting me through oo oo oo oo!

All of his notes
Above B-flat — verboten
And all of his notes
Below B-flat are rotten
Oh, Nelson
Don't call me, I'll call you oo oo oo oo!

His lovemaking casts such a pall
It's hard not to sleep through it all
His vocal chords carry
Insurance by Lloyds

And so, might I add
Should his adenoids

The lights wilt his hairdo
On camera he'll primp
And, quite frankly, his hair
Isn't all that goes limp
Darling, Nelson
How incredibly boring
That's not singing, that's snoring!

What you're putting me through

The picture of strength
And good breeding of course
And of passion and warmth
(I'm discussing his horse)
Darling, Nelson
Don't call me, I'll call you oo oo oo oo oo oo oo!

The picture of virtue and class
"America's Sweethearts" my ass
A pair made in heaven
The fans used to say
But each time we kissed
I'd swear he was gay…

In film after film after film
I betrothed him
We snuggled and smooched
And, oh God, how I loathed him
Dear Nelson,
Oh so calming
You'll never need embalming
Oh Nelson
What you're putting me through
      oo oo oo oo oo oo oo oo!

JERRY'S GIRLS

Sung to the tune of "It's Today" from *Mame*.

Carol Channing,
Beatrice Arthur, Ethel Merman,
Jerry's girls
There's Pearl Bailey and Bernadette Peters,
Angela Lansbury doubled her fame
The Winter Garden was sellout
When she played the hell out of *Mame*
Phyllis Diller, Leslie Uggams,
Annie Miller doin' twirls
Lisa Kirk in *Mack and Mabel*,
Ginger Rogers, Betty Grable
Are just some of Jerry's girls

Susan Hayward
Jo Anne Worley, Mary Martin,
Jerry's girls
He's had Lucie Arnaz and her mother
And Mrs. Santa Claus and Martha Raye
Mimi Benzell wooing Weede,
And Chita and Eydie Gorme
Eileen Brennan in her ribbons,
Kitty Carlisle in her pearls,
Vera Charles and Clara Weiss and
Molly Picon, Barbra Streisand
Are some more of Jerry's girls

There's Miss Gingold and Miss Sothern
And Miss Arden and Miss Prowse
He's had Dottie Lamour and Jane Russell
And Ernestina and her hoochy cooch
He's had Miss Swit and Miss Stritch
And Miss Luft and Miss Cook and Miss Gooch
Mrs. Levi, Mr. Zaza,
Mabel Normand in her curls
Oh the marquees they've ignited
We're ecstatic and excited
To be some of Jerry's girls

JERRY'S GIRLS The opening number for an all-female (orchestra too) revue of all my stuff. — J.H.

Jerry's girls Dorothy Loudon, Chita Rivera, and Leslie Uggams surround Jerry Herman. ▶

▼ *(following pages)* **1** Andrea McArdle, Carol Channing, and Leslie Uggams. **2** Walter Charles, Leslie Uggams, Jerry Herman, Carol Channing, Andrea McArdle, and Gene Barry. **3** Dorothy Loudon. **4** Margaret Wright, Pauletta Pearson, Melanie Vaughn, and Jo Anne Worley. **5** Carol Channing, Leslie Uggams, Rita Moreno, and Karen Morrow serenade Jerry Herman at the Hollywood Bowl. **6** Dorothy Loudon and women. **7** Chita Rivera and Leslie Uggams.

JERRY'S GIRLS
TAKE IT ALL OFF

Young, gorgeous showgirls sing:

Ev'ry night at the Palace Theatre as the sound
   of the orchestra starts to swell
We walk out to begin our number, and the boys
   in the balcony start to yell
They holler:
Take it all off, take it all off
"Jeez, ladies, please ladies, take it all off
Come on and show us your fabulous riches
Come and put back the starch in our britches,
   ladies
We don't want fans, we don't want doves
You won't turn us on just by dropping your
   gloves

We want the ultimate thrill of our lives
You'd grant us our wish if we showed you our
   wives
So ladies, wind it up, shake it up
Grind it up, take it all off"

*An over-the-hill showgirl, wanders on stage
and sings:*

Ev'ry night at the Palace Theatre as the sound
   of the orchestra starts to swell
I walk out to begin my number and the boys in
   the balcony start to yell
They holler:
"Put it back on. Put it back on
Jeez, lady, please lady put it back on"
They holler "Hey" with a fervor that's growing
"Please drape a flag on whatever is showing
Lady, don't touch the glove, don't drop the
   sheath
We shudder to think what there is underneath"

The bottom's a mess and the top is a fright
They'll give me two bucks if I spare them
   the sight
They holler:
"Back it up
Jack it up
Pack it up
Put it back on."

My figure has fallen, let's face it my dear
Two trampolines would make one
   good brassiere
So lady
Rip it up
Clip it up
Zip it up
Put it back on

Dorothy Loudon sings "Take It All Off." ▶

230

OUR HEARTS BELONG TO MARY

Sung to the tune of "My Heart Belongs to Daddy."

She played a nurse
She played a nun
She played a boy who was a fairy
She stopped the show
When she had to crow
So our hearts belong to Mary

She filled the house
As Preston's spouse
Her roles just continued to vary
In sailor suit
Or strumming the lute
Our hearts belong to Mary

Yes, our hearts belong to Mary
And we'd like to offer this toast
Yes, our hearts belong to Mary
She's the top, she's the best, she's the most

Every kid in kindergarten
Clapped his hands to save
Tinker Bell
So we love you, Mary Martin
Because Mary, you did it so well

Her *Dolly* played
In Vietnam
For everyone else it was scary
But she just said "Wow
Just look at the old girl now"
And our hearts belong to Mary

From Weill to Noel
From Schwartz to Cole

From goddess to sexy canary
She made sure we'd know
That re follows do
So our hearts belong to Mary

In her bustle or
Her wimple
She's a lady of many parts
So it's really very simple
Mary Martin has stolen our hearts!

OUR HEARTS BELONG TO MARY

Written for a tribute to Mary Martin. Carol Channing and I performed it. — J.H.

THAT'S JUDY GARLAND

Sung to the tune of "That's Entertainment."

A note that is really a note
Makes the song that the songwriter wrote
Seem sublime when it comes from the throat
Of Judy Garland

And how we loved watching her grow
When she had Mickey Rooney in tow
And she'd say "We could put on a show"
That's Judy Garland

She sang on a trolley and danced with Astaire
And Judy and Gene made a hell of a pair
But then she topped it, I swear
When she played a girl named Esther
Who turned into Vicky Lester

And then, there's a night I recall
When she proved she was queen of them all
And the roof shook at Carnegie Hall
And nobody will
Compare to the thrill
Of Judy Garland

For years there's a debt I have owed
To the girl from the yellow brick road
Who could make my emotions explode
So thanks to the gods above
For letting me fall in love
With Judy Garland!

THAT'S JUDY GARLAND Written for a tribute to Judy at Carnegie Hall that I sang on stage. It's obvious from the lyric how much she meant to me. — J.H.

1 Jerry Herman (in cap) in his college production of *The Madwoman of Chaillot*.

2 & 3 Two early portraits of Jerry.

4 Jerry, Rock Hudson, Elizabeth Taylor, Ross Hunter, and Carol Channing backstage at *Hello, Dolly!*

5 Jerry reading his score to *Milk and Honey*.

6 Jerry, Robert Preston, Bernadette Peters, and Michael Stewart at *Mack and Mabel*.

7 Jerry and his good friend Michael Feinstein.

8 Jerry outside the Palace Theatre at 47th and Broadway, which was dubbed Jerry Herman Way.

9 Jerry working on "Let's Not Waste A Moment" from *Milk and Honey*.

I'LL BE HERE TOMORROW

I'll be here tomorrow

Alive and well and thriving

I'll be here tomorrow

It's simply called surviving

If before the dawn this fragile world might crack

Someone's gotta try to put the pieces back

So, from beneath the rubble

You'll hear a little voice

Say "Life is worth the trouble"

Have you a better choice?

So let the skeptics say "Tonight we're dead and gone"

I'll be here tomorrow

And tomorrow, and tomorrow

I'll be here tomorrow

Simply going on!

Herman's music and words are not just lovely;
they're also lovable. The man has never written a song in which either
irrepressible optimism or bittersweet melancholy does not spread hope
or comfort. — John Simon, *New York Magazine*

▲ Three favorite photos that didn't fit anywhere else (top to bottom): Carol helps Jerry out-of-town with *Dolly!*; Carol, Eileen and Sondra record *Dolly!* (note Sondra on 7 Up box); Angela arriving at the *Mame* opening night party.

BEN FRANKLIN IN PARIS
"TO BE ALONE WITH YOU" and "TOO CHARMING"
Music and Lyrics by Jerry Herman
© 1964 (Renewed)
All Rights Controlled by Morley Music Co.
All Rights Reserved   Used By Permission

A DAY IN HOLLYWOOD/A NIGHT IN THE UKRAINE
"JUST GO TO THE MOVIES" and "NELSON"
Music and Lyrics by Jerry Herman
© 1980 Jerry Herman
All Rights Controlled by Jerryco Music Co.
Exclusive Agent: Edwin H. Morris & Company, A Division of MPL Communications, Inc.
All Rights Reserved   Used By Permission

DEAR WORLD
Music and Lyrics by Jerry Herman
All Songs © 1968 (Renewed) Jerry Herman
All Rights Controlled by Jerryco Music Co.
Exclusive Agent: Edwin H. Morris & Company, A Division of MPL Communications, Inc.
All Rights Reserved   Used By Permission

THE GRAND TOUR
Music and Lyrics by Jerry Herman
All Songs © 1978, 1979 Jerry Herman
All Rights Controlled by Jerryco Music Co.
Exclusive Agent: Edwin H. Morris & Company, A Division of MPL Communications, Inc.
All Rights Reserved   Used By Permission

HELLO, DOLLY!
Music and Lyrics by Jerry Herman
All Songs © 1963, 1964 (Renewed) Jerry Herman
All Rights Controlled by Edwin H. Morris &Company,
A Division of MPL Communications, Inc.
All Rights Reserved   Used By Permission

except:
"LOVE, LOOK IN MY WINDOW" and "WORLD, TAKE ME BACK"
Music and Lyrics by Jerry Herman
© 1970 (Renewed) Jerry Herman
All Rights Controlled by Jerryco Music Co.
Exclusive Agent: Edwin H. Morris & Company, A Division of
MPL Communications, Inc.
All Rights Reserved   Used By Permission

HELLO, DOLLY! - Film
"LOVE IS ONLY LOVE" and "JUST LEAVE EVERYTHING TO ME"
Music and Lyrics by Jerry Herman
© 1966, 1968 (Renewed) Jerry Herman
All Rights Controlled by Jerryco Music Co.
Exclusive Agent: Edwin H. Morris & Company, A Division of MPL Communications, Inc.
All Rights Reserved   Used By Permission

JERRY'S GIRLS
"JERRY'S GIRLS," "MY TYPE," and "TAKE IT ALL OFF"
Music and Lyrics by Jerry Herman
© 1981, 1984, 1986 Jerry Herman
All Rights Controlled by Jerryco Music Co.
Exclusive Agent: Edwin H. Morris & Company, A Division of MPL Communications, Inc.
All Rights Reserved   Used By Permission

LA CAGE AUX FOLLES
Music and Lyrics by Jerry Herman
All Songs © 1983 Jerry Herman
All Rights Controlled by Jerryco Music Co.
Exclusive Agent: Edwin H. Morris & Company, A Division of MPL Communications, Inc.
All Rights Reserved   Used By Permission

MACK AND MABEL
Music and Lyrics by Jerry Herman
All Songs © 1974 (Renewed) Jerry Herman
All Rights Controlled by Jerryco Music Co.
Exclusive Agent: Edwin H. Morris & Company, A Division of MPL Communications, Inc.
All Rights Reserved   Used By Permission

MACK AND MABEL (1995 London Production)
"MACK AND MABEL" and "SO WHO NEEDS ROSES"
Music and Lyrics by Jerry Herman
© 2003 Jerry Herman
All Rights Controlled by Jerryco Music Co.
Exclusive Agent: Edwin H. Morris & Company, A Division of MPL Communications, Inc.
All Rights Reserved   Used By Permission

MADAME APHRODITE
Music and Lyrics by Jerry Herman
All Songs © 1961 (Renewed) Jerry Herman
All Rights Controlled by Jerryco Music Co.
Exclusive Agent: Edwin H. Morris & Company, A Division of MPL Communications, Inc.
All Rights Reserved   Used By Permission

MAME
Music and Lyrics by Jerry Herman
All Songs © 1966, 1967, 1968, 1973 (Renewed) Jerry Herman
All Rights Controlled by Jerryco Music Co.
Exclusive Agent: Edwin H. Morris & Company, A Division of MPL Communications, Inc.
All Rights Reserved   Used By Permission

MILK AND HONEY
Music and Lyrics by Jerry Herman
All Songs © 1961 (Renewed) Jerry Herman
All Rights Controlled by Jerryco Music Co.
Exclusive Agent: Edwin H. Morris & Company, A Division of MPL Communications, Inc.
All Rights Reserved   Used By Permission

MISS SPECTACULAR
Music and Lyrics by Jerry Herman
All Songs © 2002 Jerry Herman
All Rights Controlled by Jerryco Music Co.
Exclusive Agent: Edwin H. Morris & Company, A Division of MPL Communications, Inc.
All Rights Reserved   Used By Permission

MRS. SANTA CLAUS
Music and Lyrics by Jerry Herman
All Songs © 1996 Jerry Herman
All Rights Controlled by Jerryco Music Co.
Exclusive Agent: Edwin H. Morris & Company, A Division of MPL Communications, Inc.
All Rights Reserved   Used By Permission

NIGHTCAP
Music and Lyrics by Jerry Herman
All songs © 1958 Jerry Herman
All Rights Controlled by Jerry Herman
All Rights Reserved. Used by Permission

PARADE
Music and Lyrics by Jerry Herman
All Songs © 1960, 1961, 1969 (Renewed), 2002 Jerry Herman
All Rights Controlled by Jerryco Music Co.
Exclusive Agent: Edwin H. Morris & Company, A Division of MPL Communications, Inc.
All Rights Reserved   Used By Permission

"OUR HEARTS BELONG TO MARY" and "THAT'S JUDY GARLAND"
Lyrics by Jerry Herman
Songs © 2003 Jerry Herman
All Rights Controlled by Jerry Herman
All Rights Reserved. Used by Permission

PHOTO CREDITS

Billy Rose Theatre Collection, the New York Public Library for the Performing Arts, Astor, Lenox and Tilden Foundation

20, 24, 26, 28, 31 (right), 50, 52-53 (Photos 2, 7), 65, 81, 95 (bottom right), 127-149, 163, 169 170, 192

Friedman-Abeles
Cover, Frontispiece, Pages 7-10, 15, 27 (top), 31 left, 32, 40, 42- 44, 46-47, 52-53 (Photos 1, 3, 5, 6), 57, 71, 74-80, 82-88, 90-92, 94, 95 (bottom left), 100-123, 219-221

Kenn Duncan
184-185, 188

Margery Gray Harnick
Page viii

Joan Marcus
66-67

Photofest
Page 3, 13, 19, 22-23, 27 (bottom), 34-35, 52-53 (Photos 4, 8), 64, 93, 95 (top), 194, 197, 198, 200-202, 205

Martha Swope
175, 176, 178-181 (top), 182, 183, 186-189, 193, 222, 225

All other photos from private collections

Nightcap logo by Hal Jacobs

ACKNOWLEDGEMENTS

With endless gratitude, I would like to thank the playwrights and authors whose words have inspired my words:

Michael Stewart
Jerome Lawrence
Robert E. Lee
Harvey Fierstein
Don Appell
Tad Mosel
Mark Saltzman
Mark Bramble
Francine Pascal
Thornton Wilder
Patrick Dennis
Jean Giradoux
Maurice Valencey
Franz Werfel
S.N. Behrman
Jean Poiret

To Bob Merrill, a great gentleman who collaborated with me on the "Motherhood March" and "Elegance" my special thanks. He handed me the ideas and opening phrases of both songs, insisted on no credit, and left me to finish the songs. I felt it was not proper to include them in a collection of my work. — J.H.

Marcy Agmon
Billy Rose Theatre Collection Staff
Teddy Blonkowski
Helene Blue
Dave Bogart
Jessica Bumstead
John Eastman
Harvey Evans
Michael Feinstein
Peter Felcher
Andrea Felder
Peter Filichia
John Fricke
Sheldon Harnick
Kenneth Kantor
Barry Kleinbort
Angela Lansbury
Tom Lasanti
Bob Mackie
Terry Marler
Louise Martzinek
Jeremy Megraw
Richard Norton
Robert Sell
Michael Shoop
Robert Taylor
Special thanks to Sheila Mack for her help and enthusiasm. — K.B.

◀ Lisa Kirk, Jerry Herman, and Angela Lansbury at the opening night of *La Cage Aux Folles*.